THE PLAY PRESCRIPTION

Other Redleaf Press Books by Aerial Liese

Ants in Their Pants
Come and Play
Nature Sparks

THE PLAY PRESCRIPTION

Using Play to Support Internalizing Behaviors

Aerial Liese, PhD

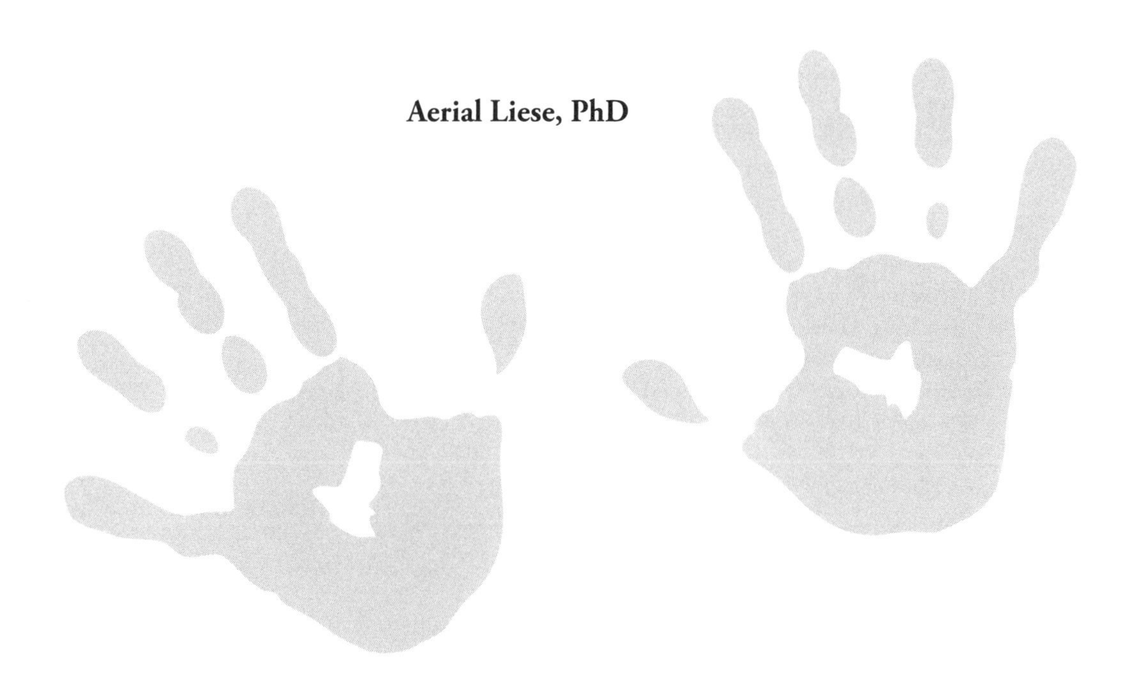

Redleaf Press®
www.redleafpress.org
800-423-8309

Published by Redleaf Press
10 Yorkton Court
St. Paul, MN 55117
www.redleafpress.org

First edition 2021
Cover design by Louise OFarrell
Cover photograph by Adobe Stock/Jacob Lund
Interior design by Becky Daum
Interior photos by Audrey Cross
Typeset in Adobe Garamond Pro
Printed in the United States of America
28 27 26 25 24 23 22 21 1 2 3 4 5 6 7 8

Library of Congress Cataloging-in-Publication Data

Names: Liese, Aerial, author.
Title: The play prescription : using play to support internalizing behaviors / by Aerial Liese, PhD.
Description: First edition. | St. Paul, MN : Redleaf Press, 2021. | Includes bibliographical references and index. | Summary: "The Play Prescription explores internalizing behaviors such as anxiety, depression, and social withdrawal found in young children, ages 3 to 7. Behavioral symptoms are discussed, with a focus on child development and emotional competence. Dr. Liese discusses a range of research-supported interventions and prevention methods for children presenting symptoms and offers clear descriptions of educational strategies and implications for educators"-- Provided by publisher.
Identifiers: LCCN 2020057212 (print) | LCCN 2020057213 (ebook) | ISBN 9781605547466 (paperback) | ISBN 9781605547473 (ebook)
Subjects: LCSH: Play assessment (Child psychology) | Child psychopathology--Treatment.
Classification: LCC RJ503.7.P55 L54 2021 (print) | LCC RJ503.7.P55 (ebook) | DDC 618.92/89--dc23
LC record available at https://lccn.loc.gov/2020057212
LC ebook record available at https://lccn.loc.gov/2020057213

Printed on acid-free paper

To my brothers, Bud and Mickey: life's adversity has changed you;
such change permitted what Fred Rogers calls "real strength."

When I was a boy, I used to think that strong meant having big muscles, great physical power; but the longer I live, the more I realize that real strength has much more to do with what is not seen. Real strength has to do with helping others.

Fred Rogers

Contents

Preface ix

Introduction 1

Part I: Fundamentals of Internalizing Behaviors

CHAPTER 1 A Guiding Framework 13
CHAPTER 2 Fundamentals of Child Development 31
CHAPTER 3 The Role of Attachment in a Child's Mental Wellness 42
CHAPTER 4 Depression in Children 58
CHAPTER 5 Anxiety in Children 65

Part II: Alleviating Internalizing Behaviors through Play

CHAPTER 6 The Cathartic Powers of Play 75
CHAPTER 7 Integrating a Diverse Play Menu 85
CHAPTER 8 Environmental Needs for Strong Mental Wellness 100
CHAPTER 9 Nature's Role in Supporting a Child's Mental Wellness 130
CHAPTER 10 Pathways to Creativity and Self-Expression 146

Conclusion 168

Helpful Handouts 169

References 173

Index 183

Preface

Play is a universal part of childhood that presents itself in myriad ways and connects to a multitude of important learning opportunities. It acts as a natural means of communication for young children, permitting the practice of emotional regulation, socialization, and other essential developmental skills. Attributes such as play's ability to propel a child's creative processes are correlated with strengthening resilience. Play has repeatedly and successfully been used in the early identification, intervention, primary prevention, and support of childhood externalizing and internalizing behaviors. That power is the focus of this book.

At their most basic level, internalizing behaviors are inwardly focused behaviors that reflect a child's negative emotional and psychological state. Unlike externalizing behaviors, which project outwardly toward others and the physical environment, internalizing behaviors are aimed inwardly—toward the self. While externalizing behaviors consist of acting out disruptively, impulsively, defiantly, and aggressively, internalizing behaviors include anxiety, social withdrawal, and depression.

Taking into consideration that internalizing behaviors left untreated in childhood can escalate into adolescence, I believe it is useful to explore internalizing behaviors carefully and individually from externalizing counterparts. Why? To better understand their early development, distinctive characteristics, and core concerns.

Additionally, because internalizing behaviors are directly connected to various negative outcomes and consequences for a child's learning and development, the early identification, intervention, primary prevention, and support of such behaviors (hereafter EIIPS) are an essential priority in early childhood programs.

Why I Wrote This Book

This book is for early childhood professionals who desire to be better equipped to meet the developmental and mental wellness needs of children experiencing internalizing behaviors. As Dr. Ken Ginsburg, pediatrician and child development researcher at Children's Hospital in Philadelphia, notes, "Play is essential to the social, emotional, cognitive, and physical well-being of children beginning in early childhood" (Milteer et al. 2012, e204). Substantial research has shown that play during the early years of a child's life is necessary if children are to reach their full potential—hence play's significance as a part of a child's day. Yet opportunities for children to play are diminishing, with many schools offering fewer play spaces, less freedom to roam outdoors, and decreasing time for free play (Yogman et al. 2018). This is unfortunate because research reveals that children benefit profoundly from daily unstructured playtime.

Harvard Medical School maintains that play is as vital to children as proper sleep and nutrition. Cathy Malchiodi and David Crenshaw assert in their book, *Creative Arts and Play Therapy for Attachment Problems*, that substantial positive correlations exist between play and the relief of many behavioral and emotional disorders (2015). Richard Louv, author of the bestselling book *Last Child in the Woods*, contends that for healthy overall development, children require spontaneous play that is free from adult directives and instead enables freedom to explore, create, and instill resilience (2008).

Nevertheless, early childhood educators face a disheartening challenge: children are becoming increasingly play deprived, and this deprivation adversely affects their physical, emotional, and psychological health. This book intends to

- add to the limited literature that is available to early childhood and mental health professionals on the topic of internalizing mental health conditions;
- provide practical, straightforward, yet creative strategies, with play as the cornerstone; and
- make professionals aware of the monumental cathartic effectiveness of play in supporting children to overcome internalizing behaviors.

My hope is that professionals who read this book will be inspired to reclaim play in children's lives to enhance not only their academic experiences but also their mental wellness, growth, and development—regardless of individual learning style, culture, economic status, or environment.

Inside This Book

The book is divided into ten chapters, which are grouped into two parts. Part 1 presents the fundamentals of internalizing behaviors and how to identify them in children, while part 2 provides practical information on using play to alleviate these behaviors.

The introductory pages define the term *internalizing behaviors* in more detail and outline the differences between internalizing and externalizing behaviors and characteristics of both as well as characteristics to consider, such as comorbidity. Terminology specific to the book and its purpose close the introduction.

Chapter 1 discusses the book's framework, the five pillars of addressing internalizing behaviors; how to identify a child's unique formula; obstacles to EIIPS; and the child development models that serve as the book's theoretical road map.

Chapter 2 examines background knowledge important in considering a child's mental wellness, such as adverse childhood experiences (ACEs) and developmental milestones and circumstances.

Chapter 3 looks at topics of attachment and emotional self-regulation and their importance in child development.

Chapters 4 and 5 delve into two of the most common childhood internalizing behaviors—depression and anxiety—and outline their characteristics and action signs. These chapters also discuss social withdrawal, which, unlike depression and anxiety, is not a clinically defined disorder in childhood, but rather is viewed as a symptom of the two other conditions. Social withdrawal is also viewed as a catalyst for depression and anxiety that frequently escalates both conditions in severity and leads to associated characteristics, such as peer rejection, bullying, poor self-esteem, and difficulties forming healthy relationships. Although not given its own chapter, social withdrawal is a central and characteristic theme that weaves throughout the text.

The chapters in part 2 are organized according to topic. Chapter 6 reviews play's cathartic powers and the use of a prescriptive tool kit and accompanying adaptive tools. Chapter 7 discusses the value of a diverse and integrated play menu and supplies numerous play ideas and strategies. Chapter 8 identifies environmental characteristics that promote strong mental wellness in children. Chapter 9 outlines nature's cathartic role in effectively addressing internalizing behaviors and how stakeholders can incorporate it into children's play. And chapter 10 focuses on pathways to creativity and self-expression, such as drawing, music and movement, sensory pathways, and more.

Finally, the book offers a set of helpful, reproducible handouts available online. These handouts are practical advice meant to be shared with families and stakeholders working with children experiencing internalizing behaviors. Added resources and references are also given on each handout for further study on the topic. Although at times the ideas overlap for creative and adaptive purposes, they are presented in a concise, easy-to-read format for stakeholders to quickly and simply understand and apply in any environment. The information presented in this book is intended to be pragmatic, adaptable for children in any sphere of influence, and able to support countless conversations with families about their children's mental wellness, overall development, and unique formulas.

How to Get the Most Out of This Book

Through play, children acquire confidence, develop trust, forge friendships, expand language, discover belonging, and learn to regulate emotions. This book supports the philosophy that to address and support childhood internalizing behaviors, a prescription for a return to play is required. But not just any play—the rambunctious and exuberant play that promotes creativity, resilience, and self-control. Play that goes beyond the rigid parameters of organized games. Active play, especially outdoor play—which helps alleviate childhood obesity and social isolation, to which excess screen time is a contributing factor—that shows children it's all right to fall and scrape their knees and not fear failure. Play that teaches children to take chances because in doing so, innovative ideas are sparked. Play that fills a child's tool kit with the healthy techniques and solutions through which children learn to regulate their emotions and handle social conflict.

The pages that follow are filled with play theory, background knowledge, activities, ideas, and tips to equip a play tool kit that supports children who are experiencing internalizing behaviors such as depression, anxiety, or social withdrawal. Such a tool kit will provide value over the course of an entire lifetime and is as vital for a child's development as learning the ABCs and 123s. Each part of this book offers useful play strategies and resources to identify the way children learn best and retain information, which will make it much easier to connect them to play's cathartic power. Once this is accomplished, educators can gauge how the child relates best to play and its diverse forms.

Additionally, *The Play Prescription* provides valuable supplemental information to reflect on in boxed form, labeled "Please Consider. . . ." The material within these boxes is meant to enhance concepts and propel further study. It may recommend a connecting storybook that enhances a concept, a list of culminating activities, a craft idea, or a simple mini-lesson on a particular subject. Anything triggering academic or sensory extensions to play may show up as a "Please Consider" suggestion.

Children are uniquely defined with formulas all their own: individual strengths, personalities, learning styles, cultures, backgrounds, life circumstances, developmental levels, family needs, and patterns of growth, risk, and resilience.

Introduction

Every child is like all *other children,* some *other children,* no *other children.*

—Clyde Kluckhohn and Henry A. Murray, Personality in Nature, Society, and Culture *(1953)*

The mental health needs of US children are growing. In particular, the needs of preschoolers with internalizing mental health behaviors are rising to a crisis level. Presently, one out of every five preschool-aged children meets the criteria for a diagnosable condition. Additionally, effective resources grounded in evidence-based research that inform and support intervention, prevention, and best practices are scarce—as are mental health professionals and educators who specialize in working with young children who struggle with these behaviors (Lipsky 2020). However, many believe, me included, that a return to play can be the antidote to childhood internalizing behaviors.

Like sleep deprivation, play deprivation has adverse consequences. Stuart Brown, MD, founder of the National Institute for Play, and play researcher Dr. Peter Gray connect childhood internalizing behaviors with play deprivation. Both experts emphasize that childhood mental health issues increase as childhood playtime decreases (Pica 2015). Social functioning, self-control, and other cognitive skills may not mature properly. When children are deprived of their right to play, serious developmental challenges ensue; while the physical effects may be more immediately apparent, the psychological problems that result deserve just as much attention, if not more.

A review of more than forty studies illustrated the cathartic power of play and found that it is significantly related to improved language skills and problem solving, increased creativity, and reduced social and emotional challenges. Moreover, considerable research has illustrated that children who have suffered adverse childhood experiences (ACEs) are further at risk of negative psychological outcomes when they lack play during and/or after those experiences (Lipsky 2020; Sahlberg and Doyle 2019).

Because play is a natural means for children to express themselves and communicate their thoughts and feelings (Axline 1947), professionals are turning to multipronged approaches to tap into its cathartic powers, accessing children's inner emotional worlds and catapulting the healing process. Play—infused with pathways to creativity and self-expression, the natural world and its elements and materials, and the use of all a child's senses—is recommended for children experiencing internalizing behaviors.

What Are Internalizing Behaviors?

An internalizing behavior is conduct that reflects a child's emotional and psychological state in the form of inwardly directed, overcontrolled actions. Examples include excessive sadness, worry, social isolation, and loss of interest in activities they usually enjoy. These are a child's way of signaling distress, and confronting the root source of that distress demands immediate attention. If left untreated, an internalizing behavior can significantly impact the trajectory of a child's development in multiple ways. It jeopardizes the self-confidence and social skills needed to build healthy relationships, compromises early language acquisition, and threatens both the child's health and safety and that of others.

As noted, childhood internalizing behaviors are at an all-time high. Yet relevant behavioral support materials, studies, best practices, and public knowledge continue to lag significantly behind those that focus on externalizing behaviors (Whalen et al. 2017). It is imperative that stakeholders thoroughly comprehend their differences. A chart defining and summarizing the variances between internalizing and externalizing behavior challenges appears on page 3.

Internalizing vs. Externalizing Behaviors

Consider the following scenario: Lacey, age four, is coloring with several of her classmates. Lacey's crayon breaks, and she remains stiffly seated, not attempting to reach for or ask for another crayon. Eventually, coloring time ends, and when Lacey's teacher asks her why she didn't finish the coloring page, she begins to quietly pout and nervously looks toward the floor, saying nothing. Brody, age five, is working at the same small table. When his crayon accidentally breaks, he throws it across the room and grabs a new one out of the hands of the little girl sitting next to him. Lacey displayed an internalizing behavioral response to the broken crayon; Brody, an externalizing one.

Internalizing behaviors are actions that are directed inward, or within the self. Children with internalizing behaviors typically have introverted temperaments, are

Externalizing Behaviors	Internalizing Behaviors
◆ The child deals with problems by acting out. Distress is targeted toward others. ◆ The child experiences high levels of irritability. ◆ The child's play is frequently uncooperative and argumentative. ◆ The child is persistently aggressive (verbally or physically). ◆ The child's behaviors are coercive, uncontrolled, impulsive, and at times violent. ◆ The child is prone to temper tantrums. ◆ The child is disruptive and noncompliant in class. They often defy the teacher. ◆ The child is unable to consistently follow class rules.	◆ The child deals with problems internally instead of acting out. Distress is aimed toward the self. ◆ The child is withdrawn and not interactive with other children. ◆ The child's play is solitary, and few positive social interactions are attempted. ◆ The child is unable to stand up for themselves and is overly anxious or apathetic. ◆ The child's behaviors are fearful, overcontrolled, and rigid. ◆ The child displays extreme shyness and appears sad and isolated. ◆ The child lacks spontaneity and has poor self-esteem. They often sulk, stare, or are secretive. ◆ The child has somatic complaints, such as headaches, gastrointestinal discomfort, a poor appetite, or sleepiness.

Figure Intro-1

exceedingly dependent on their caregivers, and are less likely to be identified for a mental or behavioral health screening because they do not create the havoc that frequently characterizes children with externalizing behaviors. Like Lacey, their behavior patterns are more likely to be problems to themselves than to those around them. They commonly experience feelings of loneliness, guilt, insignificance, panic, anxiety, doubt, insecurity, and sadness and are prone to perfectionism. Figure Intro-1 summarizes the differences between internalizing and externalizing behaviors.

Characteristics of Internalizing Behaviors

Preschool-aged children experience intense developmental changes that create brain pathways crucial for development and emotional health. Unfortunately, the onset of an internalizing behavior creates obstacles within these pathways. Early childhood educators play a pivotal role in the identification and prevention of internalizing behaviors. However, identifying children exhibiting internalizing behaviors is often a much larger challenge than identifying those with externalizing behaviors.

Various play strategies are available to help the child, but gaining a comprehensive understanding of a child's condition will allow stakeholders to make the most appropriate decisions regarding intervention. Being able to recognize common characteristics of internalizing behaviors allows educators to intervene early on, thus providing children the help they need in a timely manner.

Prevalence

Years ago, many professionals viewed the idea of preschool-aged children experiencing internalizing behaviors with skepticism. They questioned whether children could intellectually grasp such intense, grown-up emotions as depression and anxiety. They viewed screenings as too easily misconstrued due to the enormous growth and changes that occur during the preschool years. Some educators and mental health professionals, then and now, have held the widespread belief that children will simply "grow out" of challenges. However, research has shown that internalizing behaviors *do* occur in preschool-aged children (Biddle 2018; Szekely et al. 2018).

Clinical depression and anxiety have been confirmed in children as young as three, and diagnosis rates are increasing. Studies show that between 4 and 6 percent of preschoolers have serious emotional conditions that warrant intervention. Unfortunately, many of these children are overlooked for support services. Furthermore, research not only confirms the onset and prevalence of internalizing behaviors in preschool-aged children but also substantiates the detrimental effects they have on their development (Lipsky 2020; Whalen et al. 2017).

Comorbidities

Studies also emphasize that children with internalizing behaviors often experience comorbidity, or co-occurring conditions. For example, attention deficit hyperactivity disorder (ADHD) commonly co-occurs with childhood depression and anxiety (Lipsky 2020). When it comes to intervention, it is important to consider comorbidities due to the extensive overlap of condition symptoms. For example, features of childhood depression and those of anxiety typically walk hand in hand and frequently cause diagnostic problems. These factors must all be carefully distinguished from one another.

Similarly, when a child has an outwardly obvious disability, such as cerebral palsy or a vision or hearing challenge, educators have a tendency to focus on that disability. Consequently, the child's emotional needs are unheeded or neglected, leading to additional challenges. This is common when a child with an internalizing behavior also struggles to process sensory input from the environment. It's worth reiteration: stakeholders should have a thorough understanding of the presentation, pervasiveness, and specific patterns of co-occurring conditions associated with internalizing behaviors, including sensory processing disorder (SPD), formerly referred to as sensory integration disorder (SID).

Children who struggle with internalizing behaviors frequently have poor sensory processing abilities, which makes it challenging for them to process incoming information through their senses and influences all domains of their development. Children with SPD may appear irritable, tense, withdrawn, lethargic, or habitually sad (Biel 2017). While SPD can surface independently from other conditions, clinical diagnoses such as depression and anxiety often accompany it, causing unclear overlap and diagnosis challenges. Such challenges make it difficult to distinguish between SPD and the symptoms of depression or anxiety. If SPD is suspected to be at the root of a child's behaviors, addressing those symptoms first and then seeing what characteristics remain is recommended. For example, a child's characteristics of anxiety amplified by loud noises may disappear when they start to feel more secure in a setting that closely monitors environmental noise (Biel 2017).

Furthermore, children with internalizing behaviors who have experienced adverse childhood experiences (ACEs) frequently struggle with SPD due to suppressed sensory information stored in their bodies that is linked to their painful experiences. For instance, certain sounds and smells can cause intense physical and psychological reactions. Many of these behavioral responses to encoded body sensations are conscious or subconscious efforts by children to regulate the emotional distress coursing indiscriminately through their systems.

Unless educators are aware of a child's individual sensory processing issues, which are aspects of their unique formula, they may label children as "oppositional," "unmotivated," or "antisocial" (Biel 2017). Chapter 8 discusses the four sensory processing patterns, common characteristics of each style, and strategies to address children's sensory processing differences. For further information, visit Sensory-Processing-Disorder .com or refer to the book *The Out-of-Sync Child* by Carol Kranowitz.

Additional Terminology

The internalizing mental health conditions mentioned in this book are discussed as classified in the *Diagnostic and Statistical Manual of Mental Disorders* (*DSM-5*), published by the American Psychiatric Association. Additional terms that frame the book are used as presented in figure Intro-2. Additionally, although the book focuses on children with internalizing behaviors such as depression, anxiety, and coexisting conditions such as social withdrawal, the ideas and content are relevant, applicable, and adaptable to any child in need of support for a behavioral or emotional condition. Also, for the sake of expediency, *early identification, intervention, primary prevention, and support* will be abbreviated throughout as EIIPS.

◆◆◆◆◆

For children who struggle with internalizing behaviors, focused partnerships between families and stakeholders can increase levels of EIIPS and grant them better

Handout 1: Child Temperaments and Goodness of Fit
Handout 2: Child Temperament Scale

www.redleafpress.org /tpp/h-1.pdf

www.redleafpress.org /tpp/h-2.pdf

Effective teachers understand that compatibility of children's temperaments with the environment, also known as goodness of fit, is essential for optimal learning. These handouts review goodness of fit, the three most common types of child temperaments, and the use of a child temperament scale to gather information to support individual child temperaments.

Please consider . . .
How the Senses Affect a Child's System

Children who struggle with internalizing behaviors frequently lack the ability to take in information, process that information, and formulate an appropriate response. Such struggles cause social and emotional difficulties through increased anxiety, and motor impairments that result in functional deficits. Know the seven senses that impact a child's system:

Sight: provides visual feedback

Touch: provides tactile feedback

Taste: provides feedback via the palate

Smell: provides feedback through scents

Sound: provides auditory feedback

Vestibular: provides sense of balance

Proprioception: provides feedback about body awareness and the body's position in space

chances at building healthy skills for school success, meaningful relationships, and fulfilling lives.

According to Parents for Children's Mental Health (2013), 70 percent of childhood mental health issues can be solved using EIIPS. Regrettably, children with internalizing behaviors are especially vulnerable, given their frequently overlooked and untreated symptoms. Thus, it is critical that stakeholders endorse early childhood settings and experiences that enforce and overcome common obstacles. Although obstacles are inevitable, solid commitments for change among stakeholders can increase available resources and, therefore, the likelihood of success. Tapping into cathartic play skills is a way for children to learn to organize adverse experiences, process painful emotions at a developmentally appropriate level, and gain a sense of mastery and control over their lives that can help them forge successful peer relationships. Ultimately, resources like this book are meant to spur stakeholders in joining focused partnerships and creating a renewed interest in EIIPS that encourages early childhood environments primed for optimal development using play.

Term	Definition
action signs	Warning signs and risk factors not intended to identify a specific diagnosis per se but to prompt *action*
child	A child between the ages of three to six with an internalizing mental health condition
development	The overall progression of a child's emotional, social, cognitive, and adaptive functioning, unless otherwise specified
environment	A child's space, furnishings, and tools as well as adults and other children within that space (Mooney 2013)
family involvement	The partnering and participation of primary caregivers and family members involved in the child's life. Primary caregivers who raise children include but are not limited to the following: ◆ biological parents ◆ foster parents ◆ grandparents ◆ single parents ◆ stepparents
mental health	Mental health, also referred to as mental wellness, refers to social and emotional competence and development of children, formed within the context of their relationships, particularly their families. It comprises their ability to experience, regulate, and express emotions, to form secure attachments, and to play in their environment.
play	A cathartic function that allows children to ◆ identify, explore, and communicate feelings and thoughts; ◆ adapt socially and thwart emotional challenges; ◆ choose what, how, and how long to explore; ◆ engage in open-ended processes reliant on imagination; ◆ problem solve and strive for process, not product; and ◆ use adaptive play tools and self-expressive modalities, deemed *pathways* in this book

stakeholder	Any early childhood professional who works with children and wants to be better equipped to meet their developmental and mental wellness needs, including but not limited to these: ◆ child care workers ◆ primary caregivers ◆ regular education teachers ◆ special education teachers ◆ pediatricians ◆ mental wellness practitioners ◆ occupational therapists ◆ physical therapists ◆ policy makers ◆ outreach service and community members ◆ administrators
temperament	The way a child organizes, approaches, and determines how to navigate learning and existing within the environment

Figure Intro-2

Part I

Fundamentals of Internalizing Behaviors

A young child's playtime in the natural world serves several significant purposes, especially diverse opportunities for growth in all developmental areas.

1

A Guiding Framework

The predominant emotions of play are interest and joy.

—Peter Gray

Internalizing behaviors affect every aspect of a child's mental wellness and development, including emotional regulation, socialization, and daily executive functioning. When children start to struggle in any of these areas, they are essentially communicating, "I may need support." They are also communicating where their strengths lie, which can be useful in the process. For optimal early identification, intervention, primary prevention, and support (EIIPS), stakeholders require a guiding framework and foundational understanding of how children interact and change, both typically and when under duress, to pick up on their calls for support. Such a guiding framework is built on evidence-based best practices that establish effective interventions—those whose success is supported by numerous research studies grounded in well-designed guiding frameworks. Effective interventions also promote a range of skills.

This chapter presents a guiding framework for EIIPS as well as practical and evidence-based strategies, resources, and recommendations stakeholders can use to support children in early childhood settings who struggle with internalizing behaviors. Also included is a brief discussion on the need for continuing, consistent communication. The book's theoretical road map closes the chapter, guided by three major theories of child development: theory of a prepared environment (Maria Montessori), psychodynamic theory of play (Sigmund Freud), and theory of psychosocial development (Erik Erikson).

The Five Pillars of Addressing Internalizing Behaviors

To ensure that educators' practices effectively support children who are experiencing the internalization of mental health behaviors, this book is based around a guiding framework consisting of five conceptual pillars.

The first pillar is the idea that early identification is the most effective component of EIIPS for internalizing behaviors in young children. Stakeholders have an invaluable role in this. By identifying behaviors early, they contribute to a child's protective factors—conditions in children's lives that reduce the risk of an internalizing behavior worsening or even surfacing in the first place. Protective factors include, for example, directing children's families to resources to help them build resilience and learn social and coping skills.

The second pillar is the idea that children develop sound mental health within the context of secure attachments rooted in healthy and trusting relationships with the people actively engaged in their lives. Children learn to trust when they feel securely connected or attached to their caregiver, but those with internalizing behaviors often lack this sense of security and trust. Stakeholders can shape or reshape a child's view of the world as trusting when they consistently allow children to express their emotions safely and freely.

The third pillar is the idea that to effectively address internalizing behaviors, a child's environment requires certain essential features that support their needs—for instance, predictability and personalized sensory stimulation. This pillar is useful to stakeholders because although children may resemble one another in age and development, their varied personal attributes influence the way they maneuver through their environment. Stakeholders can support children who struggle with internalizing behaviors by building on these qualities to create an accommodating setting.

The fourth pillar is the idea that children's social and emotional development, referred to as mental wellness in this book, requires the daily and consistent use of a diverse, individualized play menu. Play is a vital part of the best curricular methods in preschool programs and crucial to a child's brain development, as each developmental domain is not exclusive but influences the others.

The final pillar is the idea that direct individualization of intervention methods coupled with a perceptive understanding of child development and each child's uniqueness leads to success. When stakeholders have a firm grasp on the stages of child development and get to know children and their families individually, they are powerfully equipped to create an environment supportive of EIIPS.

Figure 1-1 visually presents each pillar.

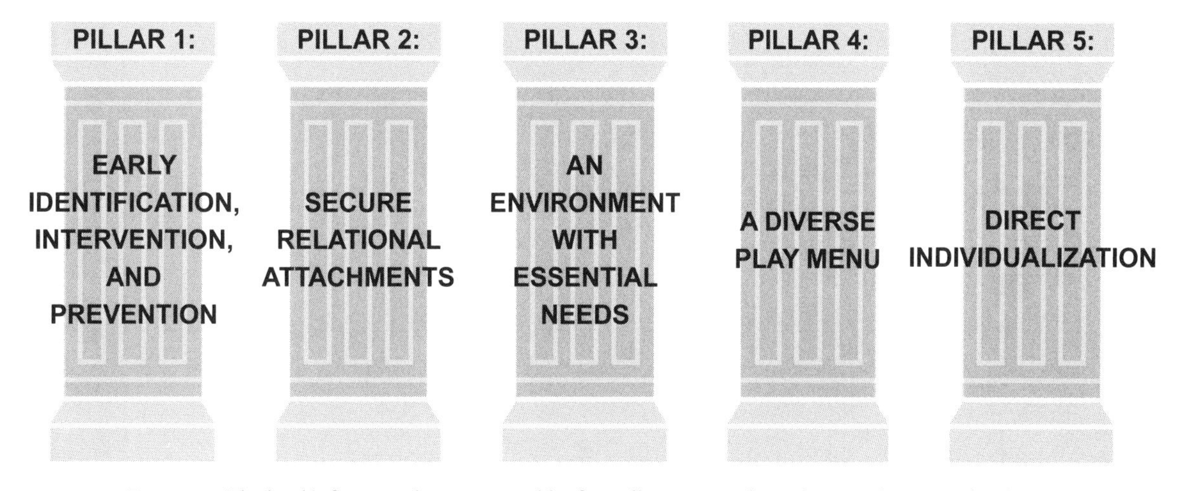

Figure 1-1. The book's framework is structured by five pillars to provide guidance and support for the book's information and strategies.

Pillar 1

Early identification of internalizing behaviors is the most effective intervention, primary prevention, and support method. Consider the following: the first three years of a child's life form a period of extraordinary brain growth and neuroplasticity. Neuroplasticity is the brain's ability to alter states, form new neural connections, and strengthen existing ones. The human brain is most malleable during the early years of life, which means that intervention during this critical period is most successful. Early identification and intervention are intended to capitalize on this window of opportunity to prevent and mitigate internalizing behaviors. Although the window remains open over the course of a child's life, neural connections become increasingly difficult to change as they age—hence the impetus for timely EIIPS.

Methods to underscore this pillar include these:

- Promote protective factors, such as developed language skills, regular physical activity, and safe opportunities, to encourage autonomy using play. Play not only improves brain plasticity but fuels protective factors (as mentioned above) such as resiliency, which in turn encourages associated skills such as emotional regulation that improve a child's overall well-being.

- Ground early identification methods in cultural and linguistic child-centeredness. For example, a child's socialization norms should be considered when designing effective family involvement strategies.

Pillar 2

Children develop strong mental health within the context of healthy relationships rooted in secure attachments. Secure attachments form when caregivers are attentive, responsive, and nurturing of children's needs. These attachments instill a sense of trust in children because they believe their caregiver will protect them. Without them, children become vulnerable to emotional and social developmental delays and language impairment. Children are more likely to develop strong mental health when stakeholders collaborate with families to build partnerships grounded in trust, security, safety, and open and effective communication. Establishing trust with a child experiencing an internalizing behavior provides a relational bond with limitless cognitive, social, and emotional guiding potential. You will learn more about secure attachments in chapter 3.

Methods to underscore pillar 2 include these:

- Stakeholders should have clarity about their role as an educator and researcher as well as have a firm understanding of child development to ground their thinking. These individuals will be equipped to work in the best interests of children with internalizing behaviors and build healthy relationships with children's families.
- Offering workshops on the importance of secure attachment and how it shapes a child's brain immediately after birth is an invaluable means of educating families. It also opens up lines of communication with families about how best to support their children.

Pillar 3

To effectively address and support internalizing behaviors, essential environmental needs should be integrated into the child's daily routine. Children's environments drastically influence their play and learning. Duncan, Martin, and Haughey (2018) write, "The [environment] is powerful. Its space has the capacity to regulate children's behavior either positively or negatively. . . . The types of materials in the [environment], including the furniture, and the way they are arranged, influence how children act, react, learn and grow" (7). Frequently, when a child is experiencing internalizing behaviors, it reflects a mismatch between their personality and setting. Oftentimes their individual needs, learning style, and temperament are compromised in some way, creating conflict. To alleviate such difficulties, provide an environment that meets children's essential needs. You will learn more about environmental needs in chapter 8.

Methods to underscore pillar 3 include these:

- Smaller play spaces within the overall setting should offer essential elements too. They should include a predictable sequence (a consistent flow that the child relies on), and any needed sensory, social, and emotional patterns should be personally prescribed for a child's energy level, mood, and socializing capability.
- A portfolio full of work samples and anecdotal notes for children with concerning behaviors is a useful data collection tool. The portfolio can support stakeholders in creating specific goals and objectives that promote child-customized interventions based on daily observations within the environment, peer interactions, and the child's strengths, unique formula, and needs.

Pillar 4

The growth of children's mental wellness is a process that requires a diverse menu of quality play, permitting cathartic pathways to creativity and self-expression. For children struggling with internalizing behaviors, a diverse play menu is essential. Quality play involves a whole-child approach, including gross and fine motor skills, senses, emotions, intellect, individuality, and social interaction. Throughout this book, you will see how play takes on a cathartic purpose—a means through which children learn to identify, communicate, and process their emotions and those of others. It becomes an avenue through which they learn to resolve inner emotional and social conflict, using adaptive play tools to learn healthy emotional regulation and social skills. This notion is framed by the psychodynamic theory of play, proposed by Sigmund Freud, who believed children can express, confront, and conquer fears and anxieties through interactive, creative, and personalized play. Using this approach to channel and convey inner distress, play takes on a form of catharsis and a means of processing and communicating for children. You will learn more about the cathartic powers of play in chapter 6. Chapter 7 considers the importance of a diverse play menu and how to integrate it into a child's environment.

Methods to underscore pillar 4 include these:

- A diverse play menu will look different in different early childhood environments because what play looks like differs among children and their circumstances. For example, children tend to embed elements of their culture into their play, revealing family beliefs and aspects of their home life and language.

- Stakeholders should regularly self-analyze and reflect on how they view a diverse play menu. Like children and their families, stakeholders' beliefs, values, and experiences (especially how they played as children) shape the way they present and nurture play.

Pillar 5

Direct and individualized support for a child's internalizing behavior goes hand in hand with a perceptive understanding of a child's unique formula and what is true about child development. Direct individualization considers the ways in which stakeholders individually respond to, interact with, and support children. It explores the uniqueness within children and the personalized modes of learning and playing that are most effective for them. It factors in exclusive patterns regarding their abilities and interests and what research states is developmentally appropriate for them. For example, movement is many young children's preferred means for learning—children retain 80 percent of what they experience physically and sensorially. Thus, a child's environment and daily routine should reflect this. Direct individualization accommodates a child's personal development, referred to as their unique formula. You will learn more about identifying a child's unique formula below.

Methods to underscore pillar 5 include these:

- Communication is key for direct individualization, as conflict can arise between stakeholders and families regarding attitudes, beliefs, and approaches toward play, learning, and situating a child's environment.
- To remain sensitive and encouraging to children's personal needs, practice purposeful observation. Jot down notes of children's day-to-day responses to happenings within the setting. Make a habit of having lunch with children among their peers, and take notice of interactions between them. Also, as much as possible, stay knowledgeable about children's individual home situations—for example, be aware if a child's parents are divorced and they alternate weekends with the child.

Identifying a Child's Unique Formula

A conceptual model of mental health and recovery also frames this book and links abstract concepts with specific support strategies. For contextual purposes, I will refer

Please consider . . .
Ways to Let a Child Individually Shine

Children who experience internalizing behaviors frequently struggle with poor self-confidence. There are numerous ways to build children's self-worth and help them realize they were meant to shine:

- Give each child a special week within the school year—preferably the week of their birthday or close to it. Children with summer birthdays can have their special week during the first or last month of the school year.
- Provide a special chair and crown for birthday celebrations. Let the birthday child sit in the chair while everyone else sings "Happy Birthday."
- Give each child a chance to shine by validating accomplishments with detailed encouragement. For example, "Wow! You did that puzzle all by yourself! You didn't give up!"
- Children also get a chance to shine when their work is attractively displayed around the room. Displaying children's work builds confidence and promotes a sense of belonging.

to the model semantically and purposely as "a restorative healing process" rather than a recovery model. A restorative healing process is relevant, practical, and useful for children experiencing internalizing behaviors, because it considers what is in the best interest of the child, according to their unique formula, and enables them to draw upon intrinsic motivation, free choice, and personally directed play to overcome their condition.

Explicitly defined, a child's unique formula is their natural manner and presence—the child's special way of being. It incorporates every individual feature that enables them to fully participate in, play, explore, learn from, and adapt to their surroundings. It consists of all those peculiarities that enable them to stumble upon what Mihaly Csikszentmihalyi calls "flow"—that delightful state of total absorption in an experience in which nothing else seems to matter (2008).

The unique formula involves personal talents, abilities, preferences, and how a child uses and sustains learning, playing, and functioning in the environment. It is also made up of their everyday experiences, culture, background, life circumstances, temperament, developmental levels, family needs, social and emotional strengths and weaknesses, and patterns of risk and resilience.

For those who work with children and want to be better equipped to meet their developmental needs, being able to recognize unique formulas is essential. Stakeholders who can identify unique formulas can prevent children from being pushed down ill-fitting developmental paths and can gain valuable insight into factors that influence the child's behavior. Picking up on a child's unique formula tendencies and cues allows professionals to incorporate into their environment what children need for healthy development. For example, Manuelito, a tactile learner (see sidebar) whose favorite

Handout 3: Multiple Intelligences and Learning Styles

www.redleafpress.org
/tpp/h-3.pdf

Using Howard Gardner's multiple intelligences can promote development and nurture a child's unique formula. Ideas to nurture the multiple intelligences are listed on this handout along with a chart presenting each intelligence according to learning style.

color is red, requires additional movement to concentrate during circle time. To meet Manuelito's needs, his teacher lets him bounce on a big red exercise ball toward the back of the room during circle time to help him focus.

Obstacles to Early Intervention and Support

The preschool years are an enormously complicated and dynamic period that can pose challenges and misunderstandings due to the rapid change underway in every area of a child's development. Consequently, obstacles to EIIPS frequently arise. As mentioned, one common obstacle is lack of training and awareness regarding how to handle internalizing behaviors in children, which unfortunately can cause well-intentioned stakeholders to unintentionally trigger stress reactions that exacerbate conditions in children. The high percentage of children who have experienced adverse childhood experiences (ACEs) demands that stakeholders have a fundamental understanding of the neurophysiological processes that occur in children who have endured significant stress.

Equipped with this understanding, it is possible to prepare appropriate environments where children feel safe to learn, play, and successfully manage their emotions.

Please consider . . .
Howard Gardner's Multiple Intelligences

Give children opportunities to nurture their uniqueness and express it through special talents and individual abilities. Consider the thoughts of Howard Gardner, who encouraged those who work with children to present information using diverse, multiple intelligences. Gardner refers to an intelligence as a child's individual ability to solve problems and learn (Bowker 2020). Children may have strengths within several intelligences—identifiable by their sensitivity, preference, and usage to retain information. Possibilities include the following:

- linguistic—learning through spoken and written language
- logical-mathematical—learning by reasoning and problem solving
- visual-spatial—learning with images and pictures
- naturalistic—learning via nature, its elements, and exploration within it
- interpersonal—learning by connecting to and with others
- intrapersonal—learning through self-identity and awareness
- musical—learning by musical patterns, rhythms, performances, and expressions
- bodily-kinesthetic/tactile—learning through movement and the use of one's body

These multiple intelligences call attention to the different ways children express themselves. Also important: discovering their true passions is another critical strategy for helping children cope with stress and learn to self-regulate.

However, defining and determining internalizing behaviors is a complex task in and of itself because the form and function of children's behaviors (within the context of their unique formulas) and the way those behaviors are interpreted depends on and is influenced by several variables. These variables include the child's developmental level,

Common Obstacles to EIIPS

Variable	Effect on Behavior
Developmental level	◆ A child's level of development (current, daily functioning) influences the way stakeholders interpret behavior. Pinpointing and describing any developmental delays a child has allows a deeper understanding of questionable behaviors. ◆ A decrease in symptoms is not an adequate measure of cathartic growth. Instead, a suitable measure should be the child's progression as compared to the typical level of development for their age.
Environment	◆ A child's daily environment affects the way a behavior is interpreted. What is appropriate in one setting may be considered inappropriate in another setting. ◆ Unidentified and unmet sensory needs within an environment can cause a child to act out. • For instance, a child sensitive to sound may be unable to concentrate or socialize when there is a high-pitched buzzing caused by faulty equipment in the background.
Family and culture	◆ A child's family and culture influence behavior. ◆ Some children have family cultures that enforce being reserved and silent in public settings, while other families encourage active socialization. ◆ Disproportionately quiet children may not be experiencing an internalizing behavior but rather may be reflecting their family culture.
Individuality (unique formula)	◆ In some instances, a child's behaviors are adaptations stemming from their unique formulas, such as background and life circumstances. • A child may "play" aggressively because older siblings model the behavior at home. • A child may express unusual but non-impairing behavior characteristic of their individuality. • A child who loves a specific type of play may become bored and unmotivated to interact with peers when placed in a setting that fails to offer this type of play.
Timing of behavior	◆ The timing of a child's behavior can also be an obstacle. • For example, a child's complete withdrawal from activities while at school could be viewed as defiance or depression unless one knew the child was being bullied by peers and only trying to avoid anxiety-provoking situations.

Figure 1-2

age, and environment; timing of the behavior; family diversity and culture; and, as just mentioned, stakeholder knowledge, experience, and training.

A child's mental wellness (emotional functioning) should be viewed through a developmental lens. This means that the child's developmental level influences what stakeholders in the child's environment deem typical or not typical, appropriate or inappropriate, or acceptable and unacceptable. For example, one typical and commonly accepted preschool-aged behavior that is also frequently misunderstood as an internalizing behavior is how a child reacts when being separated from a caregiver. A diagnosis of separation anxiety disorder (SAD) is given only when the child's anxiety and distress during separation are inappropriate for the child's age and impairs his or her functioning given their developmental level.

Separation anxiety is a usual occurrence at early stages in development that influences a child's conduct, but it typically disappears around the age of three. It is imperative that caregivers differentiate concerning behaviors from typical childhood developmental behaviors to be sure that a child's behavior is not the result of modifiable delay in development. When stakeholders are clear on the distinction, they are better equipped to work with children's families in pinpointing possible concerns that may require early intervention.

Another notable obstacle is a lack of clear eligibility guidelines, screening tools, communication, and coordination between community diagnostic and intervention services among stakeholders, including screening programs that involve families (Hodgkinson et al. 2017). This obstacle also encompasses a lack of knowledge, training, and material focused on EIIPS. Level of impairment is a significant factor to consider when referring a child for an evaluation; to warrant referral, the child's behavior must be impairing to the point of impeding their social, emotional, or cognitive development. However, this can be subjective—something that appears problematic to a teacher in one setting may not be deemed so in another setting by a family member.

Furthermore, inconsistency within variables also creates challenges in developing specific criteria and definitions that address EIIPS. To eliminate as many obstacles as possible, when defining and determining a child's behavior, the evaluation questions here should be considered in deciding whether a child should be referred for an evaluation:

- How long has the child been experiencing symptoms?
- If symptoms are recent, are there any obvious precipitating factors, such as a recent move or family discord?
- Has there been a sudden change in the child's personality or an abrupt regression in skill level?

- How are the symptoms specifically affecting or impairing the child? At school? At home? Socially with peers?

Sending home a questionnaire for caregivers to fill out is also a way to gather information about a child.

Handout 4: Sample Family Questionnaire

www.redleafpress.org/tpp/h-4.pdf

This example questionnaire encourages caregivers to list and explain in detail information helpful to stakeholders in catering specifically to children's unique formula.

The Need for Effective Communication

According to the US Department of Health and Human Services Office of Disease Prevention and Health Promotion, programs and committees guided by US and worldwide organizations have been established to begin advocating and initiating awareness about escalating childhood mental health concerns. Guiding points for committees such as the Scientific Advisory Board and the Executive Committee of the Grand Challenges in Global Mental Health include creating policy specific to child mental health, reducing inconsistencies within those policies, and using evidenced-based practices to guide them.

As emphasized on pages 177–78, consistent communication among stakeholders that all parties can easily understand—regardless of background, culture, or education—is needed. Unfortunately, communication challenges and inconsistencies remain commonplace in public education, the foster care system, and early childhood programs. This complicates the process of distinguishing characteristic symptoms of internalizing behaviors from typical preschool-aged behaviors (Whitney and Peterson 2019).

The risk factors and warning signs detailed in this book, referred to as *action signs*, are intended to help stakeholders identify children struggling with internalizing behaviors. These action signs are not intended to identify a specific diagnosis but rather to signal that *action* is needed. When stakeholders identify multiple characteristics of an internalizing behavior in a child's daily functioning, it is recommended that they act in the child's best interest pertaining to EIIPS. Action signs are invitations from a child for stakeholders to amplify the child's voice. Stakeholders can help children to become

Please consider . . .
The Goal of Mental Wellness Evaluations

The aim of a mental wellness evaluation is to provide an overall snapshot of a child's development to determine what support services are in their best interest. The screening process involves gathering cumulative information about the child from several sources, including the following:

- family interviews
- teacher comments
- observations by peers
- medical records

Notes about how children maneuver through their day and environmental tendencies that stem from their unique formulas are also beneficial. For each child, it is suggested that stakeholders develop a portfolio that includes a variety of items for evaluation purposes, such as these:

- a running log of daily comments, concerns, and quotes from the child
- descriptions of social interactions with peers
- dated work samples, such as artwork

Please keep in mind that evaluations are collective—a single observation or test score should never have the final say for a child's mental wellness evaluation.

Handout 5: Effective Family Communication

www.redleafpress.org /tpp/h-5.pdf

This handout outlines recommendations for stakeholders to practice consistent and effective communication with children and their families to build healthy home-school relationships and promote ongoing family involvements.

autonomous participants in their recovery process and empower them to build confidence, gain competence, and reestablish the lost control that is often observed alongside concerning behaviors.

A Theoretical Road Map

A theory is an organized system of principles and explanations that guide findings and answer questions. Theories on child development describe a lens through which stakeholders understand child growth and development. Stakeholders should familiarize themselves with not only one but several theories of child development and their

Key Theoretical Principles		
Maria Montessori Theory of a Prepared Environment for Play	**Sigmund Freud Psychodynamic Theory of Play**	**Erik Erikson Theory of Psychosocial Development**
◆ Children require an orderly, beautiful, sensorial environment. ◆ The environment should be full of many opportunities to move and explore. ◆ Optimal play, emotional stability, and mental focus occur when children are free to pursue their interests. ◆ Play is a child's work. ◆ For the best "work" to occur, the environment must have essential dimensions (see page 28).	◆ Children's early experiences and relationships significantly impact development and behavior. ◆ Children take play seriously and, if allowed, expend lots of energy on it. ◆ Children master skills through play. ◆ Play is a cathartic means of releasing and transferring painful memories and uncomfortable feelings. ◆ Play behavior is symbolic and driven by emotions.	◆ Play is a natural mode of self-healing for children. ◆ Play helps children progress through developmental stages and skill mastery. ◆ Each stage of a child's development has unique needs. ◆ A child's needs must be mastered before moving on to the next stage. ◆ How caregivers respond to a child in each developmental stage determines whether the child succeeds or fails in that stage.

Figure 1-3

concepts in more detail. The rationale: the combination of several perspectives supports understanding: (a) the complex and rapid changes that occur during the preschool years; (b) how internalizing behaviors impact a child's development and mental wellness; and (c) why play, secure attachment, nature, creativity, and self-expression within a prepared environment are critical and cathartic components for working with children struggling with internalizing behaviors.

The information in this book is framed within three major theories of child development: theory of a prepared environment (Maria Montessori), psychodynamic theory of play (Sigmund Freud), and theory of psychosocial development (Erik Erikson). The complexity of children's struggles with internalizing behaviors means stakeholders must understand key concepts and best practices based on knowledge, not assumptions, of how children learn and develop. These three theories provide a road map for the strategies outlined within each of the chapters that follow by drawing on principles of child development. Given this bedrock, it is my hope that the theories and best practices guiding this book will enhance and inform your work with children and support the building of stronger early childhood education programs. Figure 1-3 summarizes the key points of each theory.

Please consider . . .
The "How" and "Why" of Theories

Although EIIPS aspects grounded in theory are important, so too are how and why they are done. Theories of development secure the framework, or the "how" and "why" pieces of supporting a child. Keep in mind when working with children that something that is a preferred strategy for one theory might not be preferred according to another theory. It is also imperative to consider the following:

- Healthy child development is progressive. Children must master one level of development before moving on to the next.
- What is "best" during that level depends on each theory and a child's unique formula.
- Multiple aspects must be factored into the equation (Mooney 2013).

Theory of a Prepared Environment for Play—Maria Montessori

Many early child development theories emphasize the powerful influence of play on a child's development. However, this book uses Maria Montessori's philosophy as a theoretical framework because she considered play "the work of the child" and contended that for ideal development, the environment must include what she called *essential dimensions* for children to do their best work. For example, the environment must allow consistent, creative movement; provide choice; and foster competence and security. These essential dimensions, or essential needs, are outlined in detail in chapter 8. According to Montessori, a child's development depends heavily on an environment's preparation; she promoted child-centered, sensory-stimulating settings that are aesthetically appealing, methodically arranged, and full of pleasant aromas, rich textures, and interesting sounds. Furnishings and play tools are child-sized to perfectly fit little hands and bodies.

In Montessori's view, the educator's primary duties in preparing the environment are (a) to set up an individualized system where children, regardless of physical ability, are free to move about and to and from activities; (b) to emphasize the natural world as an extension of classroom lessons; (c) to provide children with ample time, tools, and choices for deep and uninterrupted exploration of play; and (d) to provide children with a sense of security, communicated by an environment being consistent, structured, and run by routine. Montessori also strongly believed the environment should encourage family involvement, because children are subconsciously taught from their home environment as well.

Psychodynamic Theory of Play—Sigmund Freud

Sigmund Freud also stressed the significance of play on a child's mental wellness, emphasized its cathartic value to support and improve a child's emotions, and considered play a useful means of transference. For example, he highlighted that through play, children create safe contexts to confront anxiety-inducing events by transferring passive experiences (quiet time that may involve listening, drawing, or reading) into active ones (movement time that may involve socialization, engagement, or exploration) and permitting inner conflict to be addressed—for example, in a private loft where a child can go to calm down. Transference is discussed further on page 80.

Freud wrote extensively about play's symbolic and unconscious meaning, describing it as a "poetic creation" and postulating two major aspects of play as therapeutic: catharsis and mastery (Kidd n.d.). The *cathartic* element of play represents children's need to escape and process negative feelings that can impede their development. The *mastery* element stems from a child's need to gain emotional control over their life. Eventually, through both elements, the child regains control in play over what they may have lost control over in real life. Like Montessori's theory, Freud's *psychodynamic theory of play* is a child-centered, verbally expressive approach and is supportive of children who struggle with developmentally appropriate anxiety, depression, and poor social skills (Salcuni et al. 2017).

Psychodynamic refers to a developmentally appropriate, curative means for children to express their emotions and internal struggles (Fernandez and Sugay 2016). Psychodynamic play tools can help anxious children become more trusting and withdrawn children grow more spontaneous and self-satisfied. They are also beneficial for helping children work through poor self-image issues, such as seeing themselves as bad or unworthy—emotions that commonly are at the core of internalizing behaviors (Halfon et al. 2016).

Theory of Psychosocial Development—Erik Erikson

Erik Erikson's work is valuable to early childhood stakeholders because it illustrates how play provides a strong basis for a child's development and mental wellness. Erikson too viewed play as self-curative and as a pathway through which children can cope with emotional difficulties. Freud started the discussion about the cathartic value of play, and Erikson continued examining how and why a child can benefit from it. He furthered Freud's concept of "repetition compulsion"—a continual craving to return to familiarity, regardless of whether the familiar brings comfort or distress—hypothesizing that through play, children unknowingly reenact and reinvent their stressful experiences to understand and master them (Knight 2017).

Moreover, Erikson's *Theory of Psychosocial Development* considers the impact of external factors such as home life and parenting style on a child's development. Although both Montessori and Freud emphasized developmental stages, Erikson's theory methodically accentuates the fact that children must pass through a series of eight specific and interrelated stages, and that moving from phase to phase is dependent on completion of the prior stage (Knight 2017).

Erikson's stages are significant—particularly the initial stage, categorized as trust versus mistrust. Unsuccessful completion of this first stage of development leaves children insecure and believing they cannot trust their caregiver (or, by extension, the world) to protect them (Erikson 1950). Many internalizing behaviors and associated symptoms, such as social withdrawal, are a child's maladaptive attempts to regain some sense of control and security within their environment.

The eight interrelated stages are termed the *Eight Ages of Man.* The chapters that follow will refer to the first four stages of Erikson's theory, presented in figure 1-4, which comprise the age ranges on which this book focuses. For a detailed explanation of all eight stages, refer to Erikson's seminal book *Childhood and Society*.

Erickson's Stage of Development	Psychosocial Crisis	Approximate Age
I. Infancy	*Trust vs. mistrust:* A child's ability to develop trust depends on the degree of responsive care by caregivers.	0–1 yr.
II. Early Childhood	*Autonomy vs. shame/ doubt:* Children develop autonomy if they can assert their will and independence through making choices.	1–3 yrs.
III. Play Age	*Initiative vs. guilt:* Initiative develops when children initiate activities with direction and purpose.	3–6 yrs.
IV. School Age	*Industry vs. inferiority:* Industry develops as children pursue challenging tasks with eagerness and curiosity.	6–11/12 yrs.

Figure 1-4. Erikson's Psychosocial Theory of Development—The Eight Stages of Man (first four). Adapted from Erikson, Erik. 1963. *Childhood and Society.* 2nd ed. New York: Norton.

◆◆◆◆◆

The five pillars of addressing internalizing behaviors presented in this chapter provide a framework for stakeholders to establish best EIIPS practices within their work with children. As discussed, within this framework it is critical to specifically identify children's unique formulas and to take these formulas into account to ensure that each child is served in the way best suited to them. Bear in mind this information, as well as the child development theories of Montessori, Freud, and Erikson, as the rest of part 1 lays out the key foundational information that will allow you to effectively harness the cathartic powers of play as an expression of a child's inner world.

2

Fundamentals of Child Development

It is in playing, and only in playing, that the individual child or adult is able to be creative and to use the whole personality, and it is only in being creative that the individual discovers the self.

—Donald Woods Winnicott, British pediatrician

In her book *What If Everybody Understood Child Development?* (2015) Rae Pica asks several questions: What changes in early childhood education might occur if stakeholders considered the fundamentals of child development? How much healthier might children's lives be if stakeholders understood this unique period of their lives well? What if stakeholders grasped that children each develop at their own pace and, when forced to perform skills they are not developmentally ready to perform, become frustrated, unmotivated, and even fearful? What if stakeholders realized that when children can grapple with items of interest, lasting learning occurs?

What if stakeholders comprehended that to help children overcome internalizing behaviors, they must consider specific aspects of child development for effective EIIPS?

Chapter 1 established that an understanding of play as catharsis and a strong knowledge base of child development theory are essential features of stakeholders' repertoires. Selma Fraiberg, a pioneer in the work of early childhood development (1951), stressed that in facilitating cathartic work with a child, "our objective is to bring the child up to the level of development appropriate for his age. . . . This means, further, that a theoretical knowledge of the . . . development of children, and the developmental tasks and conflicts which come with each stage, are an indispensable part of the worker's equipment" (179).

In addition to the developmental theories that frame this book, discussed on pages 26–30, we will also draw on important background knowledge of child development for understanding that the preschool years are a crucial period for EIIPS. Topics include but are not limited to sensory challenges, adverse childhood experiences (ACEs), developmental milestones, emotional regulation, and social skills. This knowledge is meant to be incorporated in upcoming chapters as well as considered *true*—irrefutably proven to support the unquestionable connection between how children develop; how they play; and how they use play to confront, process, and address emotional turmoil.

How ACEs Impact a Child's Mental Wellness

Kevin was five years old when he began talking to his preschool teacher about his feelings. Initially, he kept her at bay with minimal dialogue, but as the days passed, Kevin was more relatable. He shared how the other children never played with him and how this made him feel lonely. During class time, when Kevin was supposed to be working on his assignments, he doodled pictures of his father lying on a couch with bottles spread all over the floor. The faces on the other figures in his drawings were always smiling, except Kevin's, which always displayed tearstained cheeks.

When Kevin's teacher met with his mother about Kevin's inability to stay on task, as well as his continual solitary play and daily drawings, the mother cried and explained that Kevin's father had lost his job, begun drinking, and withdrawn more and more from the family. She said that at one time Kevin's father was very attentive to Kevin, but within the last couple of months, he had spent less and less time with the boy. What little time he did interact with Kevin was flooded with harsh and short-tempered words. Kevin's mother admitted this was particularly hard on Kevin because months earlier he and his father had been inseparable—constantly roughhousing on the living room floor or playing catch outside.

Kevin's ordeal can be described as an adverse childhood experience. ACEs are defined as mistreatment and neglect expressed through traumatic events, such as physical, sexual, or emotional abuse; an absence of parental nurturance, affection, and attachment; parent death or incarceration; or witnessing domestic violence, household substance use, or adverse mental conditions in the home. Living in extreme poverty for extended periods of time is also considered an ACE and has been proven to have harmful effects on a child's development (CDC 2019), as has experiencing natural disasters. Children who have experienced stress during and after severe environmental trauma require developmentally appropriate mental wellness interventions, termed *psychological first aid*, due to typically recurrent nightmares, flashbacks, and depression. Other examples of ACEs are listed in figure 2-1.

According to Jia Jia Liu, Yanping Bao, Xiaolin Huang, Jie Shi, and Lin Lu (2020), the quarantining and social restrictions required during the COVID-19 pandemic may have psychological repercussions on children, including prolonged sadness, fear, and panic. Although some level of emotional unease can be expected from the unfamiliar and unexpected changes unfolding during the pandemic, stakeholders should remain cognizant of the particulars that may be driving a child's behavioral and emotional reactions to the changes. For illustration, consider that if children's caregivers model calmness and positive self-regulating behaviors, as opposed to exhibiting worry and

Adverse Childhood Experiences (ACEs)

Examples of ACEs include but are not limited to the following:

- Emotional abuse/neglect, including being repeatedly left alone for long periods of time
- Living in extreme poverty for extended periods of time and/or experiencing homelessness
- Physical abuse/neglect
- Experiencing a natural disaster or war
- Witnessing domestic violence inside or outside the home
- Household substance abuse and/or mental illness of a parent or family member
- Parental separation or divorce
- Incarceration of a household member
- Bullying by another child or adult
- Witnessing racism or discrimination

Figure 2-1

fear themselves, the child will more than likely mimic those responses. Children's abilities to regulate their behaviors, emotions, and thoughts during stressful times are significantly influenced by what is modeled by their caregivers and within their environment.

ACEs seriously impact a child's brain development, physical growth, physiology, and ability to form secure and meaningful relationships. Children who have endured multiple ACEs that began early in childhood and were frequent and continuous commonly struggle with learning disabilities and poor emotional regulation. In addition, according to a 2016 study for the New Mexico Sentencing Commission, many stakeholders have little knowledge of how to respond to the impact ACEs have on a child's ability to learn, the damaging effect of ACEs on a child's overall development, how to prevent children from developing an internalizing behavior due to ACEs, or the large number of children experiencing internalizing behaviors due to ACEs that warrant EIIPS.

Consequently, stakeholders' understanding of what ACEs are and how they impact development are central to EIIPS. Such an understanding provides a context in which to understand difficult emotional moments and behaviors that are directly related to internalizing behaviors. Furthermore, it is equally critical that stakeholders recognize that ACEs are frequently at the root of many childhood internalizing behaviors or coexisting conditions, largely because ACEs are grounded in more than the emotional matters related to witnessing or being a victim of the event.

Key to this book's focus, it is necessary that stakeholders build a collection of play-based interventions and strategies for their prescriptive tool kits that provide children a nonverbal cathartic means of self-expression. Play integrated with nature, creativity, and sensory pathways can have miraculous outcomes in reversing the damaging impact of ACEs. Part 2 digs deeper into this topic.

Handout 6: Understanding Adverse Childhood Experiences

www.redleafpress.org
/tpp/h-6.pdf

This handout discusses how adverse childhood experiences (ACEs) impair children's brain development and impede their learning.

Developmental Milestones Are Different for Every Child

As already stated, children develop at their own pace, so it is impossible to know exactly when any individual child will reach a particular milestone. Milestones are as individual as each child and uniquely matter for EIIPS. When considering a child's developmental milestones, it is important to remember four pertinent truths.

First, standardized early child development milestones are characterized by the acquisition of certain skills during the first five years of a child's life. These skills are based on *typical*, or most commonly observed, behaviors. Thus, understanding what is considered typical is useful in determining whether a child may require an evaluation, whether their developmental level may explain a behavior, and whether consideration of the *whole* child was factored into the equation. Stakeholders should review developmental milestone charts to become familiar with typical preschool-aged behaviors, keeping in mind that they will not reflect every child's progression. My own experience has demonstrated that the inconsistencies children frequently present are often differences in degree more than differences of kind.

Second, the child is an extension of a much larger unit of support—the family—and expectations around developmental milestones are commonly driven by family culture. The culture and language of the family have a significant impact on a child's development, and a child's culture is embedded in everything they do. The way in which stakeholders communicate and understand a child's family diversity and differences influences development, especially if expectations are unpredictable and incompatible with the child's culture. For example, some children are reluctant to answer a teacher's questions because it conflicts with the way they were raised. Unless the teacher understands this, such behaviors could easily be misconstrued as an internalizing behavior or related condition. Nonetheless, in daily interactions with children and their families, be mindful that culture and family priorities are influential and should be valued and nurtured for healthy relationships that encourage family involvement. Ultimately, what happens to the child happens to the family. Figure 2-2 outlines some strategies for cultural competence.

Third, all children display challenging behaviors at one time or another. The distinction between what is believed challenging versus diagnosable is based on measures of duration, age-appropriateness, intensity, and complexity. For further detail, please refer to figure 2-3.

Finally, a child's developmental strengths and weaknesses must be part of the EIIPS equation. Familiarity with children's strengths and weaknesses is essential to fostering their emerging cognitive abilities and understanding how delays or advancement

Please consider . . .
Developmental Growth Charts

Developmental growth charts are available online from the US Centers for Disease Control and Prevention (CDC). The CDC website offers a free downloadable milestone tracker mobile app that does the following:

- tracks developmental milestones
- provides helpful videos, tips, and activities
- shares explanations of when to act if a child displays questionable behaviors
- issues reminders for recommended developmental screenings

While the website lists typical milestones for preschool-aged children, the CDC and the American Academy of Pediatrics advise parents that there may be deviation from the provided timeline that remains within the bounds of typical development. It's also normal to have concerns or questions about the rate at which a child reaches these milestones. If experiencing such concerns, speak to a pediatrician or family physician to schedule an evaluation or learn more about potential developmental delays.

may be approached. Pages 39–41 go into more detail about discovering children's developmental strengths and weaknesses.

Circumstances That Influence a Child's Developmental Milestones

The circumstances of children's lives influence their behavior, play, and development. For example, children who have repeatedly moved from school to school will likely absorb learning differently than children who have attended the same school all their lives. When presented with unusual circumstances that may influence a child's developmental milestones, seek advice from the child's family, offer support when appropriate, and always make families feel welcome by using open communication and collaboration. When communication is open, discussions about life experiences and circumstances—both positive and challenging—are more genuine. Also remember

Cultural Competence Strategies

- Implement a set of values and principles that recognize diversity, including diversity of gender, nationality, language, race, ethnicity, religion, culture, and disability.
- Demonstrate behaviors, attitudes, policies, and structures that are cross-cultural.
- Conduct assessments to ensure sensitivity to cultural characteristics.
- Be committed to manage and consider what families can and cannot do.
- Learn and incorporate cultural knowledge into practices, including sources of diversity.
- Adapt to diversity and the cultural contexts of the cultures served.
- Collaborate closely with families, considering culture-based communication, such as predisposition, tone of voice, touch, and facial expression.
- Empower families with training and consider what is functional for them.

Figure 2-2

Criteria to Determine Challenging vs. Diagnosable Behavior

Duration of behavior	How long has the child had the problem? Is the child merely having a bad day, or has the behavior been going on for weeks?
Age-appropriateness of behavior	A three-year-old wrapped around Dad's leg on the first day of preschool is developmentally expected. A nine-year-old who acts this way is not.
Intensity of behavior	To what extent is the behavior disrupting the child's life? A four-year-old so afraid of monsters under the bed that they are not able to fall asleep, even after repeated reassurance, may need an evaluation.
Complexity of behavior	Despite experience and the passing of time, is the child maintaining the problem to a high degree?

Figure 2-3. Bayat 2019.

Please consider . . .
Cultural Competence

Culture impacts the way a child

- learns
- behaves
- sees the world
- responds to personal strengths and limitations

Culture includes how families teach their children to

- socialize
- choose words and tone of voice
- use body language and eye contact
- demonstrate physical boundaries

Because a child's culture heavily determines behavior, it is important to understand and respect individual cultural practices, or practice cultural competence: "Cultural competence is the ability to understand, communicate with and effectively interact with people across cultures" (Western Center for Research and Education 2017). To implement cultural competence, openly communicate with families. Try to learn as much as possible about a child's culture, which is a key step in interpreting behavior that could be at the root of an internalizing behavior.

Handout 4: Sample Family Questionnaire

www.redleafpress.org
/tpp/h-4.pdf

Stakeholders can send this sample questionnaire home with families to gather information that may be useful in catering specifically to children's unique formulas for learning and playing and serving distinct child and family needs.

that, once again, early intervention is key. It's best to identify an internalizing behavior during a child's preschool years, before it becomes unmanageable during adolescence.

If you're a stakeholder who is concerned about a child's development, troublesome behavior, or circumstances, consult an administrator. If you're a parent, contact the child's pediatrician or other health care provider. Professionals should carefully share any thoughts with the family by describing the child's behavior and the observed reasons for concern. It is helpful to write down specific, observed examples of behavioral concerns in advance, preferably referencing when, where, and in what context the behavior(s) took place. The handout Preparing for an Appointment is designed to help prepare for a school meeting or physician appointment. Use it as an outline for notes and to organize any thoughts, questions, and concerns about circumstances or otherwise.

Figure 2-4 presents circumstances that frequently influence a child's developmental milestones and must be factored into internalizing behavior intervention.

Handout 7: Preparing for an Appointment

www.redleafpress.org
/tpp/h-7.pdf

This handout encourages caregivers to take time before a child's appointment to think about what they want to discuss while there. Whether the appointment is with a pediatrician, teacher, or other provider, helpful questions, observations, and concerns to consider before the visit are outlined.

Discovering a Child's Developmental Strengths and Weaknesses

When working with children with internalizing behaviors, stakeholders should learn as much as possible about their past and present home environments to intervene appropriately, as needed. They should also be familiar with a child's strengths and weaknesses, which are key ingredients in their unique formula. Being aware of a child's developmental strengths and weaknesses serves many purposes. For one, incorporating children's strengths into play and capitalizing on their interests to overcome developmental weaknesses acts as a motivational tool for sustained learning. This awareness can be accomplished by observing and questioning the smaller details of children's unique formulas, such as those presented in figure 2-5. Children are more likely to reach their full potential if instruction and play begin at their developmental level.

If a child displays slow progress or considerable weakness in any area of development, this is not necessarily a sign of a delay. Monitor the child's behavior to see

Circumstances That Influence a Child's Developmental Milestones	
Family makeup	◆ How many people live in the child's home? ◆ Does the child live in a two-parent home, a single-parent home, or a blended family?
Birth order	◆ Does the child have siblings? How many? ◆ Where does the child fall in the birth order?
Home language	◆ Does the child speak a language other than English at home? ◆ Is the child fluently bilingual?
Socioeconomic status	◆ Does the child live in poverty or wealth?
Education	◆ How much education do the child's guardians have? ◆ How do the guardians view education?
Trauma	◆ Has the child experienced an ACE? (see page 33)
Age of parents	◆ Does the child have a teen parent? ◆ Is the child's caregiver a grandparent?

Figure 2-4

whether it worsens, and provide several opportunities for the child to creatively problem solve before intervening. Start simple and remember to capitalize on the child's strengths and interests when considering options. For example, problem solving can be as simple as redirecting a child to ask a peer a question: "Have you told Rita how it makes you feel when she doesn't share the crayons with you? Maybe Rita doesn't know that you're feeling this way."

Frequently, as a child's confidence grows in areas of problem solving, their challenging behaviors decrease and they experience more developmental success. Nonetheless, if the challenge escalates instead of diminishes over time, it may be

Questions to Discover Children's Developmental Strengths and Weaknesses

- What makes the child laugh? Smile? Get frustrated?
- What is the child's favorite play space? Least favorite?
- What captures and keeps the child's attention?
- What play tools does the child choose most often? Least often?
- When is the child most often immersed in a state of "flow," as described on page 19?
- To or from what activity does the child struggle to transition?

Figure 2-5

helpful to seek a second opinion and discuss whether an assessment for the behavior is warranted and an intervention appropriate.

◆◆◆◆◆

A child's cognitive, emotional, and social development are entwined. Together they lay the groundwork for a young child's future. Therefore, many aspects of development must be considered when supporting a child struggling with an internalizing behavior. Aspects of co-occurring conditions, poor sensory processing patterns, and a child's developmental strengths and weaknesses should all be factored into EIIPS. At the cornerstone of interventions should be play. Playtime *plays* a significant role in a child's development and mental wellness because it provides limitless access to a child's thoughts and feelings. For children struggling with internalizing behavior symptoms, various forms of play are essential for cathartic purposes.

Understanding this chapter's discussion on ACEs, their impact on a child's brain development, and how they are linked to internalizing behaviors and can significantly impede a child's learning (Holmes et al. 2015) is necessary before moving on to chapter 3. ACEs tremendously impact a child's development, and stakeholders should be knowledgeable of them to implement effective EIIPS. The next section discusses how the application of varied play is a key component of addressing internalizing behaviors. The different types of play that should be incorporated in a child's environment to master developmental skills like emotional regulation and socialization are discussed. Numerous suggestions for each play form to fill stakeholders' prescriptive tool kits are also provided.

3

The Role of Attachment in a Child's Mental Wellness

Try to see [a] child as a seed that came in a packet without a label. Your job is to provide the right environment and nutrients and to pull the weeds. You can't decide what kind of flower you'll get, or in which season it will bloom.

—A modern educator (quoted in Mogel 2001)

Secure attachment is a first critical milestone for establishing sound childhood mental wellness. Secure attachments allow a child to trust that their caregiver(s) will protect them and keep them safe, an initial stage of development grounded in Erikson's *Theory of Psychosocial Development*, outlined on page 29. Attachment also plays a critical role in emotional regulation for a child experiencing an internalizing behavior, because children gradually learn that even though they are feeling a certain way, they have a secure base (their caregiver). This secure base offers a safe haven where they can move back and forth for comfort, protection, and emotional replenishing.

The quality and stability of a child's early relationships are foundational for many aspects of psychological development, including establishing healthy self-esteem, intrinsic motivation, impulse control, and social skills. When children do not experience early secure relationships that are warm, affectionate, validating, and consistent, their brain development suffers, which impedes learning and play and increases emotional problems.

Furthermore, the basic architecture of a child's brain is constructed through an ongoing process that begins before birth and continues into adulthood. Early experiences and relationships affect the quality of that architecture, establishing either a sturdy or a fragile foundation for a child's future mental wellness. Children's abilities to regulate and express emotions and to develop strong social skills, which enable them to establish close relationships, are cornerstones of their mental wellness. However, before they can achieve these competencies, children need to feel a strong and secure sense of connection, or *attachment*, to their environment and the relationships within it. When this requirement is met, children develop self-confidence and trust both their surroundings and the people in it. When it is not, they are prone to internalizing behaviors.

Additionally, secure attachments buffer children from other stressors that could otherwise lead to internalizing behaviors. It is common for insecurely attached children to be angry, socially awkward, unconfident, and withdrawn. They also struggle to regulate their emotions and frequently perform poorly in school. On the other hand, children with secure attachment typically blossom socially and emotionally and flourish in school, among other traits (see figure 3-1). One reason for this is that securely attached relationships help children feel confident in seeking out emotional intimacy with others during times of stress, allowing them to resolve that stress rather than turning it inward in the form of internalizing behaviors.

Securely attached relationships form when caregivers are consistently sensitive, attentive, and responsive to children's needs as well as able to developmentally understand and support them. For instance, while we can expect an older child to sit still for long periods, we should not hold a three-year-old to this same standard. Receptiveness to the child's needs comes through an ongoing exchange of verbal and nonverbal communication in various forms, including direct eye contact, relaxed and open body language, and a warm and affectionate tone of voice. As children emotionally and physically tune in to this enduring and genuine exchange of communication, they learn to feel safe, secure, and accepted by their caregiver.

Securely Attached vs. Insecurely Attached Children

Children who can regulate their emotions are typically better able to concentrate and more prepared to learn. Children's ability to regulate their emotions has repercussions across all areas of development, and those who have learned to appropriately control their feelings also learn to correctly identify and label them: for instance, "I'm mad because Johnny won't let me play with him!" At the same time, as children grow, they improve on their abilities to manage their emotions to match the situation and environment. For example, a child separates from a parent to attend a friend's birthday party for two to three hours, realizes the caregiver will return, and does not lose emotional control.

Children who struggle to regulate their emotions typically shut down and withdraw. They have difficulty staying on task, completing work, calming themselves down when agitated, following rules, finding successful solutions to problems encountered with peers, and transitioning between places, activities, and people. Children who are not able to appropriately regulate their emotions are hesitant to enter situations in which they are separated from their caregiver, such as going on a playdate without their caregiver. They often require specific guidance on how to enter and exist in these everyday situations. Ultimately, children who struggle to appropriately regulate their emotions require direct instruction of support strategies.

Characteristics of Securely Attached Children

- The child enjoys and pursues interaction with others.
- The child seeks help from others when needed.
- The child shows affection toward others.
- The child is confident.
- The child is trusting of the environment and the people within it.
- The child is glad to see parents and stakeholders when they return from an absence.

Figure 3-1

Please consider . . .
Children without Consistent Caregivers

Children raised in institutions, foster care systems, and group homes where a primary caregiver is not present are often unable to appropriately regulate their emotions. Many more of these children develop internalizing behaviors as compared with children raised in nuclear families with consistent primary caregivers. Children raised in these environments may also have additional concerns:

- becoming socially withdrawn, apathetic, and depressed
- displaying inappropriate friendliness with strangers
- developing unhealthy attachments with any authority figure who shows interest in them
- exhibiting noticeable social challenges by the age of four or five
- experiencing problems with concentration
- having a propensity for extreme temper tantrums

Secure Emotional Regulation and Mental Wellness

Emotional regulation is a child's ability to control bodily functions and impulses, manage intense feelings, and maintain focus. Studies show that the emotional competence of young children is significantly more advanced than previously presumed. Children can experience and learn to regulate surprisingly deep and strong feelings. During the preschool period, they develop emotional regulation, self-expression, and strategies for identifying and understanding emotional states—all of which influence relationships and social skills. An essential facet of emotional regulation for children with internalizing behaviors is learning which strategies to use when confronted with an uncomfortable feeling.

Children experience emotional dysregulation when they do not know how to express an emotion, instead suppressing it because they have not learned to identify and manage it. Consequently, that emotion will randomly well up in them during a stressful situation. It is important for stakeholders to understand that a child who suppresses a feeling is not in control of it. Children are typically referred for EIIPS when they have such struggles with regulating their emotions.

Strategies to Improve a Child's Emotional Regulation

Although children are constantly honing their abilities to manage uncomfortable feelings, they still require considerable guidance and practice in developing a strong and sound set of emotional regulation skills. Stakeholders play a critical role in the development of this skill set, giving children a secure emotional and relational base they can seek out and draw from for support. This base also supplies tools the child can use to manage difficult feelings.

Numerous methods are available for stakeholders to use to teach children to effectively progress in regulating their emotions. One effective method is make-believe play. This type of play is directly linked to emotional regulation: when a child plays out an uncomfortable emotion or event using make-believe, the separation between reality and fantasy is emphasized, and a bridge between communication and understanding is built. Figure 3-2 lays out other approaches to help children develop strong emotional regulation skills.

Handout 8: Strategies to Develop a Child's Emotional Regulation

www.redleafpress.org /tpp/h-8.pdf

This handout reviews strategies to develop a child's emotional regulation. The ideas are also designed to increase a child's energy, stimulate development, and improve mood, and they can easily be modified according to a child's unique formula, implemented into lessons, and shared with parents in a newsletter sent home.

Mental Wellness Requires Strong Social Skills

Children experience their world through relationships. The early patterns of these relationships influence their social development and contribute to building competencies, such as intrinsic motivation (initiative from within that is driven by internal rather than external rewards), strong self-worth, and healthy emotional regulation. Healthy socializing for children means making and maintaining friendships and actively engaging in social interactions without the use of verbal or physical aggression. It requires them to learn to regulate their emotions and develop an interest in their environment—an interest that will be made apparent by the child's willingness to form relationships with the individuals in it.

Strategies to Develop a Child's Emotional Regulation Skills	
Strategy	**Examples**
Model expected behaviors	◆ Children learn from watching their caregivers. Thus, set an example of expected behavior. ◆ Model step-by-step self-talk as expectations of behavior are carried out. ◆ Use deliberate and purposeful verbal explanations.
Create the environment's behavior expectations as a class	◆ Work with children to propose and create the behavior expectations for each environment. ◆ Role-play acceptable and unacceptable actions. ◆ Help children internalize expectations via modeling and self-talk. ◆ Be sure children can verbalize the "why" of expectations. For example, "We share because we decided it is kind to share."
Encourage positive behaviors with visuals	◆ Use concrete visual prompts, such as pictures, to encourage children to meet behavior expectations. ◆ Use positive reinforcement with these visuals, remaining attentive that positive reinforcement should immediately follow the appropriate behavior and be implemented in incremental steps toward behavior improvement. ◆ Try out a variety of visual supports, remembering that they are meant to help children work, play, and think more independently. Visuals can take many forms, including these: • charts and diagrams: visuals that hang in the environment for everyone to see and use • mini charts/diagrams: smaller visuals for an individual child based on personal needs • props: objects that prompt a specific action or thought for a child • visual reminders: a sticky note or index card with a personal word or picture to remind a child of something • pictures: a photograph that positively portrays a child in a moment of work or play that stakeholders want to reinforce

Integrate activities that are repetitive	◆ Rhythmic tasks encourage emotional regulation by requiring children to focus on the process, promoting relaxation and supporting the ebb and flow of a child's thoughts. Examples of repetitive activities include these: • threading colorful, different-sized beads to make a necklace or bracelet • gardening tasks, such as preparing soil, weeding, trimming, digging, sweeping, or harvesting
Teach conflict resolution	◆ Teach conflict resolution and prosocial skills in anticipation of disagreements. ◆ Create specific play spaces, both indoors and out, that help children practice communication and problem-solving skills. ◆ Read and discuss books that highlight how people work through differences, which supports the development of a culturally rich, sensitive, and peaceful environment.
Incorporate fantasy and sensory play	◆ Provide play opportunities that allow children to speak and act out scenarios in third person. ◆ Use play such as puppetry to allow children to rehearse emotional regulation skills through role play, projecting their emotions, and pretending. ◆ With supervision, let children work with balloons. Whether bursting, releasing, stretching, decorating, or tossing, balloon play is a creative, sensory, and physical means of self-expression that cultivates emotional regulation. ◆ Set up sensory break areas, tables, or bins where children can go to refocus when they feel overloaded.
Use games and activities	◆ Play charades as a class and have children dramatize words. For example, act out words such as *embarrassed*, *bored*, *angry*, and *lonely*. ◆ To enhance the game, discuss and role-play ways to cope with such feelings. Ask questions like these: • "Have you ever felt this way?" • "What made you feel like this?" • "What do you do when you feel this way?" ◆ Here are some additional childhood games that promote emotional regulation: • Mother, May I? • Red Light, Green Light • Statues • Freeze Tag • Simon Says

Engage children directly with nature	◆ The calming effects of nature provide countless opportunities to help children regulate, channel, and process their emotions, including digging in sand, building forts, and lying on the ground looking up at the sky. ◆ Being outdoors enables physical activity, which eases tension and reduces anxiety. Physical activity such as hiking or walking around the playground stimulates the release of feel-good endorphins. ◆ For a child with an internalizing behavior, the solitary experience of creating and working in a personalized garden can be greatly beneficial in regulating feelings.
Provide structure and guidance	◆ Provide as much structure as possible in scheduling and transitioning and within the physical environment. Structure the setting for a child's success. Stakeholders should not repeatedly be telling children no. ◆ Post a daily, visual, and consistent yet flexible schedule. Post simple, positive rules to help structure a child's day. ◆ Structure should challenge skills and set limits, using creativity and being considerate of children's unique formulas (see pages 18–20). ◆ Scaffolding is a part of guidance. Provide the appropriate amount of guidance for children to develop skills.
Establish trust	◆ Children learn emotional regulation when they trust their caregivers and environment. These strategies help to establish trust: • anticipating needs based on reading verbal and nonverbal body language • answering requests in a timely and consistent manner • validating emotions and modeling empathy and compassion • following through reliably with statements and setting consistent, age-appropriate boundaries

Build emotional literacy	◆ Help children build their emotional language to identify and express what they are feeling and why. Discuss appropriate versus inappropriate expression of emotions through interactive reading and storytelling. ◆ Interactive verbal activities, such as rhyming, telling riddles, making silly sounds, or singing new lyrics to familiar songs can help develop a child's emotional vocabulary and can be incorporated into storytelling. ◆ Integrate creative pathways such as drawing and painting into play and story activities to accomplish goals. ◆ Help children develop a full spectrum of feelings, using specific words to express and describe their emotions and experiences—both negative and positive. For example, explain, describe, and role-play anger, disappointment, frustration, excitement, and eagerness. ◆ Use visual supports, including emotion charts, cards, and wheels, which are beneficial in supporting and increasing children's receptive and expressive communication.
Model empathy	◆ Like other expected behaviors, children learn empathy when they see their caregivers model it by accepting and responding to others' emotions with compassion.
Offer physical support	◆ If a child is on the verge of losing emotional control, be their regulation tool by physically moving toward and redirecting them. ◆ Get on the child's level, make eye contact, display open body posture, listen, and speak in a soft tone with a slow and even tempo.
Redirect the child	◆ Redirect a child who is struggling to follow rules. For example, "Let's go to the block area and help Juan build a tower." ◆ It's helpful to phrase redirection as a problem-solving question. For example, "What do you think would happen if you shared the blocks with Juanita?"
Affirm the child	◆ Practice repeating positive affirmation orally. For example, "I can do my best." ◆ Praise children when they demonstrate improved or appropriate emotional regulation. ◆ Model thinking out loud and help children recognize triggers when they may be going down an ineffective and negative path of thinking. ◆ Discuss and role-play examples of turning negative thinking into positive thinking.

Use relaxation and breathing techniques	◆ Teach children relaxation strategies to calm down, reduce anxiety, or refocus negative energy. For example, try visualization: Turn off the lights to create a calming mood. Have children sit in a comfortable position and close their eyes. In a quiet voice, describe to them a pleasant, relaxing scene, such as playing with puppies or kitties or receiving a birthday present. The scene described should be appropriate to the children's age and development. Play music or nature sound recordings in the background. ◆ Read stories such as *Little Cloud* by Eric Carle to help children visualize relaxing images, such as being a fluffy cloud. Sensory play can be added—for example, have children use shaving cream or whipped cream to draw the shape of the cloud they visualized. ◆ Play Pretzel: Have children stand or sit and wrap their arms around themselves, slowly twisting their bodies like pretzels, while breathing in and out to selected music. ◆ Children often respond well to scents like lavender, an herb that naturally promotes relaxation. ◆ To help children calm themselves, sprinkle scents throughout the environment. Let children work with a sensory substance that incorporates scent, such as pounding clay scented with vanilla or chamomile.

Figure 3-2

All of this is possible when secure and healthy relational attachments are formed by means of consistent nurturing and support from stakeholders. A child who experiences regular responsive and affectionate caregiving is more likely to have a positive self-image and want to socialize with peers. Children who lack the social competence to interact with their peers are prone to numerous difficulties, such as social withdrawal, social isolation, peer rejection, loneliness, and a lack of genuine friendships. Stakeholders need to support children who struggle to appropriately socialize through directly teaching them strategies to learn how to do so.

Strategies to Strengthen a Child's Social Skills

Numerous methods are available for stakeholders to use to develop a child's social skills. Many of the suggestions in figure 3-2 are applicable, such as using make-believe play, which is directly linked to helping children learn to socialize. For example, as children take on roles during house play, they converse to *play* the part. Figure 3-3 presents further recommendations.

Additionally, remember to offer children a diverse play menu, which not only helps develop social skills but establishes relational attachments and sound emotional

Please consider . . .
Prompts to Support a Child's Emotional Regulation

When redirecting children to support their emotional regulation, consider the use of indirect verbal, gestural, or direct spatial prompts:

- **Indirect verbal prompt:** Ask a question to prompt positive behavior. For example, to prompt lunch preparations: "What do we need to do now that we are back from playing outdoors?"
- **Gestural prompt:** Use body language to encourage good choice. For example, to redirect a child without calling attention to them, motion with a wave or nod.
- **Direct spatial prompt:** Place an object that directly leads a child to make a good choice. For example, place a pencil directly in front of a child and say enthusiastically, "It's time to work on writing our names."

regulation. Offering children numerous forms of play to hone socialization boosts independence, self-confidence, and empathy. Chapter 7 discusses various forms of play in depth accompanied by suggestions for social skill development using each form.

Strategies to Develop Healthy Social Skills	
Strategy	**Examples**
Teach listening skills	◆ Help children master basic listening skills, such as maintaining focus on the speaker. ◆ Have children takes turns introducing one another and asking one another questions. Use props such as microphones.

Develop conversation skills	◆ Role-play conversations with children and help them improve conversational skills. ◆ Model appropriate volume, tone, and inflection. ◆ Teach and discuss how talking to others involves not interrupting them while they are speaking.
Explain nonverbal communication	◆ Use visuals such as books, pictures, and posters to help children learn the significance of body language. ◆ Role-play appropriate and inappropriate gestures and facial expressions.
Use positive reinforcement	◆ The goal of positive reinforcement is to intrinsically motivate a child, demonstrated when children engage in an activity for its own sake and not because of continual extrinsic rewards. ◆ Intrinsically motivated behaviors cultivate creativity, independence, flexibility, and spontaneity, all of which are helpful for children struggling with internalizing behaviors. ◆ Positive reinforcement works best to improve social skills when it follows a consistent system of incentives, such as special privileges (for example, passing out papers). ◆ Pay close attention to what motivates a child, and use your discoveries to build a positive reinforcement system to nurture the child's intrinsic motivation.
Model kindness	◆ Model to children the importance of kind words and actions. ◆ Talk about how kind words and sincere compliments can make others feel good and build friendships. ◆ Encourage and model random acts of kindness. ◆ Discuss with children how acts of kindness made them feel.
Role-play	◆ Role-play and discuss alternative ways of interacting in social situations that let the child consider actions from the perspective of others. • Discussion helps children reflect on their actions and the feelings that often drive them. • Discussion also helps children build a richer emotional language.

Help children learn empathy	◆ Children often act and speak insensitively without understanding the effect their actions can have on others. Discuss with children how unkind words and actions can make others feel. ◆ Ask children questions about times when somebody hurt their feelings. ◆ Use books with persuasive and specific narratives to help children recognize the feelings of others.
Nurture interaction with the outdoors	◆ Create outdoor areas where children can interact and play with nature elements. Stock a place such as a gazebo with notebooks, sketch pads, various writing utensils, books, and tools such as binoculars. ◆ Set up a crafting table outdoors using objects from nature. For example, pick flowers to press onto paper, let children crush berries to make "paint," or gather pine cones and rocks to decorate. ◆ Build a bird feeder or flower box that can be placed in the environment.
Teach anger management skills	◆ Discuss and role-play appropriate ways to deal with anger. ◆ Teach students basic calming techniques, such as deep breathing. Use books to discuss the importance of expressing feelings appropriately. ◆ Have a plan in place for times when children are upset and need to refocus themselves. For example, designate a specific area of the room with a rocking chair and soft pillows.
Model "I" messages	◆ Provide children with "I" messages and other specific language they can use to communicate with peers. For example, "I feel sad when you don't share with me or give me a turn."
Build self-esteem	◆ Praise children's individual strengths and give consistent positive feedback and reinforcement for competent socialization among peers. ◆ Use musical activities to increase a child's self-confidence. For example, teach a child to play a musical instrument. ◆ Teach creative problem solving. When children experience success in solving their own problems, competence and self-esteem increase. ◆ Refrain from comparing children to one another. ◆ Display children's work throughout the environment.

Retrain thought patterns	◆ Help children to identify negative thoughts or distorted beliefs and to question and replace them with positive self-talk. ◆ Model what a child could say to themselves to be less scared in a frightening situation. This empowers them to problem solve and develop a repertoire of affirmations. • If a child experiencing anxiety expresses that they can't do something, walk them through their inaccurate thinking and help them rephrase their thinking. For example, "I can ask for help if I feel like I need it." ◆ Walk children through "calming" questions like these: • What am I worried about? • Why does it worry me? • What are the chances it will happen? • What proof do I have that it will happen? • What else could happen? • What if it does? • How can I handle it if it does happen?
Emphasize cooperative play	◆ Place emphasis on cooperative play with peers in the environment and organize the setting to facilitate it. This can be valuable to children with poorly developed social skills. • For example, incorporate age-appropriate books and interactive reading and storytelling into cooperative play spaces to support, encourage, and enhance prosocial behaviors.
Buddy up children	◆ Remember that the way stakeholders structure tasks can support or hinder a child's success. Intentionally partner children for play activities that reinforce social skills. Base partnerships on strengths, language skills, conceptual understanding, and temperament. For example, implement a play activity that requires taking turns and sharing.
Focus on connecting with, not correcting the child	◆ Spend time interacting with children when they begin experiencing intense, "big," and uncomfortable feelings. ◆ Invite multiple means of interaction and expression, including words, movement, creations, and performances. ◆ Keep in mind that to fully support children, stakeholders need to see a child's behavior as a means of communication and focus on the reason behind it.

Expose children to a variety of new social experiences	◆ Give children opportunities to experience new people, places, and activities to help them discover new interests and ways to interact. ◆ Take field trips, incorporate different types of music, books, and food options into the children's day, and invite speakers from around the community to share their jobs.

Figure 3-3

Handout 9: Fostering Intrinsic Motivation

www.redleafpress.org
/tpp/h-9.pdf

Motivation is either intrinsic (from within) or extrinsic (from external influences). Children learn best when they're intrinsically motivated. This handout presents ideas to promote intrinsic motivation that can be shared in a newsletter sent home to families or implemented in the environment.

Please consider . . . Implementing a Center Stage

Build a "center stage" to help children develop and practice social skills using creative props. Center stage is an extension of fantasy play onto a stage, such as a raised platform. As discussed throughout this chapter, playing out experiences and working through fears are important elements of play for children struggling with an internalizing behavior.

- Center stage should include an assortment of dress-up clothes and accessories. For example, create a microphone by putting a tennis ball on a thick stick.
- Contact dance schools or theater companies and ask for donations of old or discarded costumes.
- Enlist volunteers from families to build scenery.
- Create diverse settings, such as a firehouse, a marina, or a farm.

◆◆◆◆◆

Attachment is a fundamental aspect of children's emotional wellness and establishes how they see the world and the relationships formed within it. Strong relational connections—secure attachments—guide a child in developing social skills and emotional regulation. Cathartic play helps children develop these secure attachments as well as build strong social and emotional regulation skills that support children in overcoming internalizing behaviors.

Early childhood is an enormously influential period of a child's development. If children's daily experiences with their caregivers are inconsistent and detached, they are left vulnerable to the onset of an internalizing behavior. The tools in this chapter emphasize the foundational importance of attachment and how to prioritize deep, nurturing connections with children.

4

Depression in Children

One is reminded of Plato's dictum that the most effective kind of learning is that the child should play among lovely things.

—Aubert J. Clark

Wally is a bright four-and-a-half-year-old with an expansive vocabulary who, for the last six months, has shown frequent sadness and irritability with minor frustration when his preferences are not met. For example, he withdraws from eating and interacting with his peers when he does not get his favorite cup at snack time. Wally complains of regular tummy aches and demonstrates poor concentration. When outdoors, he is afraid to take risks, engages mainly in solitary play, struggles with self-expression, and lacks the stamina to sustain play with peers.

Wally's mother disclosed that he has undergone changes in his typical sleeping and eating patterns, sleeping a lot more and eating a lot less. She also disclosed that she has struggled with depression herself but said her pregnancy with Wally was free of complications. Wally is an only child from a single-parent home with considerable custodial conflict and confrontation between his parents. Observation has revealed that he neither offers comfort to his caregivers or peers nor seeks it from them. Wally's profile provides a typical picture of child depression. His somatic concerns and loss of appetite are suggestive markers. His loss of spontaneity to play and socialize with his peers are more nonspecific signs (CDC 2019).

This chapter is devoted to identifying characteristics of depression in children, action signs, and support strategies for stakeholders while building upon and integrating the essential points of previous chapters. It will also highlight social withdrawal, which is a pervasive characteristic of depression due to its interference with other areas of typical child development. Consequently, social withdrawal frequently reinforces the

Known about Wally

4.5-year-old, bright, frequent sadness/irritability, single-parent home, parent depression, separation issues, poor self-image, obsessive behavior of nail biting

Specific Questions about Wally

- *Sensory issues:* Do specific noises, tastes, textures, or smells bother Wally? At what point has Wally had enough sensory stimulation? How does he make this known?
- *Activity level:* How active is Wally? What is his degree of typical energy and movement?
- *Diet and sleep patterns:* Does Wally have predictable sleeping and eating patterns?
- *Approachability:* Does Wally withdraw from peers or readily join in with them?
- *Adaptability:* How does Wally respond to new situations?
- *Emotional response:* How does Wally express and manage his feelings? Does he have intense meltdowns?
- *Mood:* Does Wally have a positive or negative outlook? What is his overall and typical mood?
- *Distractibility:* How long is Wally's attention span? Does Wally struggle with transitioning?
- *Persistence:* How long will Wally sustain a task when frustrated?

Figure 4-1. Questions to determine Wally's unique formula when considering his characteristics of depression.

condition and escalates other symptoms, such as poor self-esteem and anxiety (CDC 2019), the latter of which is discussed in more detail in chapter 5.

Refer to figure 4-1 for an overall snapshot of Wally's inner world and questions that would be useful in determining what is in his best interest regarding EIIPS. Remember that any screening and evaluation process involves gathering cumulative educational and family information about the child from as many sources as possible and incorporating multiple levels of analysis from the sources.

Background Information

Depression requires EIIPS to avoid serious and debilitating effects on a child's development and long-term negative mental health conditions. If left untreated, depression can impact every aspect of a child's development. Children as young as three are at risk for depression, particularly when their mothers also suffer from the condition. Recent research has focused on describing, identifying, and confirming detailed, developmentally appropriate diagnostic criteria that professionals can apply to preschool children. Currently, however, there is not a definitive method of testing for early childhood depression (CDC 2019).

The current *Diagnostic and Statistical Manual of Mental Disorders* (*DSM-5)* is not well adapted for young children. Stakeholders have suggested adjustments to make the criteria more pertinent to young children. These include a developmental adjustment to the death preoccupation symptom—for example, "persistent engagement in activities or play themes with death or suicide" (Whalen et al. 4).

Lessening the duration criteria is another recommendation. The *DSM* requires that symptoms persist for a minimum amount of time in order for an individual to be diagnosed with certain conditions, but many durations are developmentally inappropriate for young children. For instance, a six-month duration for a three- or four-year-old represents a significant proportion of that child's life and therefore may not be an appropriate threshold.

Stakeholders must be knowledgeable about the characteristics, action signs, and co-occurring behaviors commonly associated with childhood depression—such as sensory processing disorder (SPD) and attention deficit hyperactivity disorder (ADHD)—to appropriately refer children for EIIPS as soon as possible. They must also understand that specific characteristics of depression may be confused with co-occurring conditions, and the underlying depression may be overlooked. Characteristics of depression can assume a myriad of unexpected forms, including many of the characteristics of anxiety discussed in chapter 5. Combinations of characteristics of both depression and anxiety are staggering, subtle, varied, masked, and idiosyncratic, and even the most trained stakeholder may miss them. However, figure 4-2 outlines some common characteristics to look for.

Common Characteristics of Depression and Anxiety in Children	
Inability to support and reaffirm self	◆ Children who are depressed and anxious struggle to reinforce their strengths and feel all right about rewarding themselves.
Learned helplessness	◆ Children who are depressed and anxious have trouble establishing a sense of control and mastery. ◆ They often consider themselves helpless, struggle to problem solve, and are unmotivated to change.
Negative self-talk	◆ Children who are depressed and anxious frequently make critical statements about themselves. ◆ They also harbor a deep sense of pessimism and feelings of uselessness.
Social deficits	◆ Social withdrawal usually accompanies depression and anxiety, which significantly diminishes social interactions. ◆ Children who are anxious and depressed often find intense social contact challenging, threatening, and hard to sustain.
Forgetting how to play	◆ Children who are depressed and anxious are typically uneasy and dissatisfied with life. ◆ It may appear that these children have forgotten how to play—as if they have lost their sense of spontaneity.

Figure 4-2. Adapted from Whalen, Sylvester, and Luby 2017.

Discovering Depression in Children

Depression has been described as a whole-body illness because it involves changes not only in mood and socialization but in many physical aspects of the person's life, such as sleep, appetite, and energy level. As mentioned, other conditions often co-occur with childhood depression, and a child's limited ability to verbalize their emotions related to the symptoms they are experiencing is a primary challenge of EIIPS. Stakeholders play vital supportive roles in EIIPS, as many characteristics are easily overlooked unless closely observed. For instance, children frequently articulate being "bored" as an alternative to expressing sadness.

Other common characteristics of depression in children include tearfulness, irritability, and a lack of joy. To distinguish depression-related behaviors from a child's typical moods, it is important to understand a child's unique formula (see page 18). Additionally, it is important to distinguish between behaviors deemed "challenging" and those deemed "diagnosable," as based on the measurable conditions discussed on page 37. Listed here are characteristics of depression in children and how they may present themselves.

Physical and somatic complaints: Children who are depressed often complain of having stomachaches, headaches, difficulty breathing, or other ailments for which there are no physical explanations. They may have repeated school absences and frequent visits to the nurse's office for these complaints. Children who are experiencing depression also commonly have disproportionate changes in their appetite and sleeping patterns.

Poor emotional tolerance: Children who suffer from depression have a diminished ability to "bounce back" from disappointment or other intense feelings. This may resemble hypersensitivity in the form of easily hurt feelings or crying when separated from a caregiver. Poor emotional tolerance of frustration may also present itself as behaviors or reactionary moods characterized by anger outbursts when the child fails to get their way.

Irritability: Irritability is a key marker of depression in children and coincides with low tolerance of frustration. It may present itself as working slowly due to distractibility and restlessness, not being able to follow through on tasks due to forgetfulness, isolation from peers during play, or difficulty socializing. For example, for children who are experiencing depression, extreme irritability frequently makes them inattentive, which in turn leads to aggression toward peers.

Sadness and loss of pleasure: Another specific marker of more severe depression in children is a lack of joy. Children who are depressed tend to have negative- and sad-themed play. They often appear lethargic and unenthusiastic toward activities that their peers find enjoyable.

Sleep disruption and poor nutrition: A disruption in eating and sleeping patterns has been shown to be a characteristic of depression in children. Children with depression commonly eat less nutritiously to self-medicate. Consequently, a diet that lacks nutrient-rich foods commonly leads to nutritional deficiencies linked to depression. For example, low levels of folate, zinc, and magnesium are inversely connected to depression (O'Neil et al. 2014).

Action Signs

As described on page 24, *action signs* are risk factors or warning signs that indicate to stakeholders when or whether to act when a child's behavior becomes questionable or is at immediate risk of developing into something more serious. Action signs are intended to prompt stakeholders to gather cumulative educational and family information about the child to create a well-informed snapshot and, if needed, to seek a full and appropriate mental wellness screening. Several characteristics elevate a child's risk of developing depression. Many of these risk factors are related to both depression and anxiety in children, further complicated by the high rates of coexisting conditions between anxiety and depression in this age range.

Family history: Children who have a learning or behavioral disorder or a family history of mental health challenges are at an increased risk for depression. It is also well documented that family members struggling with depression are typically less able to provide nurturing and secure caregiving, increasing the likelihood of a child's risk for depression.

Poor early attachment: Unstable and adverse early relationships in a child's life contribute to insecure attachments (see page 44), which also put a child at risk for depression. Poor attachments characteristically leave children feeling helpless, unloved, and without value, all of which can lead to depression (Lecompte et al. 2014).

Temperament: A child's temperament directly affects their relationships, their daily functioning, and the ways they are treated by others. As a result, children with cantankerous temperaments are at risk for depression. Temperament types are discussed on page 170.

Giftedness: Children with advanced intellects commonly are self-critical, have high standards for themselves and others, and are idealistic, having unrealistic expectations that their performance will be high all the time in everything. Gifted children's high cognitive functioning and tendency toward perfectionism, sensitivity, and social isolation are risk factors for depression (Webb et al. 2016).

Adverse childhood experiences (ACEs): Children who live in capricious, dysfunctional, or economically challenged families are at a greater risk of developing depression. ACEs such as divorce significantly influence a child's mental wellness and may contribute to a child's frequent illnesses, stomachaches, headaches, and depression. For more information on ACEs, see chapter 2.

Social withdrawal: Children who are depressed have difficulty making and maintaining friendships. They often feel misunderstood, irritable, and worthless, which fuels their desire to isolate—which perpetuates the condition.

◆◆◆◆◆

Children of all ages can suffer from depression. If overlooked, the condition can have long-term effects on how they perceive themselves and their abilities, both of which influence their future development and mental wellness. While contemplating EIIPS strategies for a child such as Wally to overcome depression, remember that many factors interact in complex ways to determine whether a strategy will be successful for the child—hence the importance of factoring in the child's unique formula. For example, Wally presents with irritabilty and lack of motivation to play and interact with his peers, all of which may require time and attention. Also deserving emphasis for Wally is learning to build healthy emotional regulation and social skills.

Consistent and diverse play and peer interaction as a means of support to refocus and pull Wally from his depressed state may prove to be invaluable for EIIPS. Additionally, because research demonstrates that medication is not the most effective option for young children who struggle with depression (Luby et al. 2018), EIIPS that target creative pathways and self-expression and that rigorously involve the child's family are recommended. When stakeholders act on a child's depressive symptoms in a timely manner, it can change the trajectory of their life and their ability to play, learn, and develop healthy friendships.

5

Anxiety in Children

Sometimes my happy gets stuck.

—Quoted in Play Therapy with Traumatized Children *by Paris Goodyear-Brown (2010)*

Jessica is six years old and suffers from a persistent fear of being separated from her mother. After arriving at school, her mother gives her repeated hugs and kisses and states that she is leaving. However, instead of leaving, her mother hangs up Jessica's coat, a task Jessica should do. Jessica continues to cling to her mother as her mother assures her that she will be back and promises not to be late. Jessica's mother moves toward the door several times, and each time she does, Jessica cries. The teacher informs Jessica that she can sit near him if she needs to but must let her mother leave. Jessica finally sits down with a lowered head and remains silent for most of the day.

Rather than engage in play with her peers, Jessica glances at the door and complains of a stomachache. During a parent-teacher conference, Jessica's mother informs her teacher that Jessica is having a hard time settling down for sleep, has nightmares about school, and throws severe temper tantrums that often escalate to biting and kicking when she anticipates separation from her mother. She also reports that Jessica shows no interest in playing with other children or visiting her father, who left soon after Jessica's birth.

Jessica's profile provides a typical picture of separation anxiety disorder with associated social phobia. Being distracted from play because of her worries and fears, having difficulty sleeping, and needing excessive reassurance are all characteristics of anxiety. This chapter is devoted to identifying the characteristics and action signs of anxiety in children and providing support strategies for stakeholders, while building upon and integrating the essential points of previous chapters. As with depression, social withdrawal is a pervasive characteristic of anxiety due to its interference with many areas of typical child development, including social skills.

Refer to figure 5-1 for an overall snapshot of Jessica's inner world and questions to determine what is in her best interest regarding EIIPS. Remember that any screening

Known about Jessica

6-year-old, single-parent home, intense meltdowns, withdrawal from peers, difficulty sleeping at night, nightmares

Specific Questions about Jessica

- *Sensory issues:* Do specific noises, tastes, textures, or smells bother Jessica? At what point has Jessica had enough sensory stimulation? How does she make this known?
- *Activity level:* How active is Jessica? What is her typical degree of energy and movement?
- *Diet patterns:* Does Jessica have predictable eating patterns?
- *Adaptability:* How does Jessica respond to new situations?
- *Emotional response:* How does Jessica express and manage her feelings?
- *Mood:* Does Jessica have a positive or negative outlook? What is her overall and typical mood?
- *Distractibility:* How long is Jessica's attention span? Does she struggle with transitioning?
- *Persistence:* How long will Jessica sustain a task when frustrated?

Figure 5-1. Questions to put into context Jessica's unique formula when considering her characteristics of anxiety.

and evaluation process involves gathering cumulative educational and family information about the child from as many sources as possible and incorporating multiple levels of analysis from the sources.

Background Information

Anxiety is the most frequently seen internalizing behavior in children and is prevalent in children as young as three (Rose 2020). Several types of anxiety conditions can be found in children: separation anxiety disorder (SAD), panic disorder, social phobia, obsessive-compulsive disorder (OCD), post-traumatic stress disorder (PTSD), and generalized anxiety disorder (GAD). SAD, GAD, and social phobia are thought to be the earliest-onset childhood forms of anxiety (CDC 2019), and this chapter will focus on EIIPS strategies for these three conditions. Figure 5-2 describes and defines characteristics of these most common anxiety conditions.

Furthermore, anxiety, like depression, requires EIIPS to avoid serious and debilitating effects on a child's development and long-term negative mental health conditions. Stakeholders must be knowledgeable about the characteristics, action signs, and co-occurring behaviors commonly associated with childhood anxiety—such as SPD, ADHD, and depression—to appropriately refer children for EIIPS as soon as possible. Per the *DSM-5*, in order for the anxiety a child experiences to qualify as diagnosable, its characteristics must be out of proportion to the actual danger or threat in the situation, after taking cultural contextual factors into account. A six-month duration is required as well.

Discovering Anxiety in Children

As is the case with childhood depression, a primary challenge of EIIPS for children experiencing anxiety is their limited ability to verbalize emotions related to that anxiety. Stakeholders play vital supportive roles in helping a child experiencing anxiety, as many features are easily overlooked unless closely observed. As noted in chapter 4, children frequently articulate being "bored" as an alternative to expressing sadness. Anxiety may also express itself in children as heightened irritability and a constant need for reassurance.

Here again, it is important to be aware of a child's unique formula and typical moods as well as the distinction between "challenging" and "diagnosable" behaviors (see page 37). Listed are further characteristics of anxiety in children and how they may present themselves.

Physical and somatic complaints: Like children experiencing depression, children who are anxious often complain of having stomachaches, headaches, difficulty

Characteristics of Anxiety Conditions in Children	
Separation anxiety disorder (SAD)	◆ Children with SAD experience developmentally inappropriate anxiety when confronted with separation from a caregiver, and it causes significant impairment in their daily functioning. ◆ Anxiety due to separation is considered typical for young children but turns problematic when the anxiety becomes excessive, intense, and frequent or continues beyond what is considered developmentally appropriate for children.
Generalized anxiety disorder (GAD)	◆ GAD is present when a child exhibits excessive and uncontrollable worry. ◆ With GAD, the child continually seeks reassurance in two or more situations or relationships. ◆ For diagnosis, at least one physical symptom must be present, such as restlessness, fatigue, difficulty concentrating, irritability, muscle tension, or sleep problems.
Social phobia	◆ A child may have social phobia if they experience persistent, unreasonable, and excessive fear of a specific object or situation (or anticipation of the object or situation) that results in an immediate response of panic, crying, tantrum, freezing, or clinging. ◆ This response causes the child to avoid the triggering situation, and the family may enable avoidance, which leads to further impairment of the child, family functioning, and the child's development.

Figure 5-2. As outlined in the *Diagnostic and Statistical Manual of Mental Disorders (DSM-5)*, published by the American Psychiatric Association (APA).

breathing, or other ailments for which there are no physical explanations. They may have repeated school absences and frequent visits to the nurse's office for these complaints. They often experience disproportionate changes in their appetite and sleeping patterns, sickness in the morning, and general muscle tension in their bodies.

Extreme attachment: Early signs of separation anxiety in children include extreme attachment, excessive worrying about being away from a caregiver, and fear of being alone. Children experiencing anxiety frequently cry excessively when away from caregivers and are likely to have difficulty making and maintaining friendships.

Insomnia and difficulty sleeping: Children who struggle with anxiety commonly experience insomnia and have trouble falling or staying asleep. They also experience nightmares and other sleep-related problems, which in turn lead to associated challenges such as irritability and poor concentration.

Sensory Issues That Frequently Accompany Anxiety

- The child chews or smells everything.
- The child is bothered by bright lights.
- The child prefers to walk on tiptoe.
- The child does not like their hair brushed.
- The child does not like being barefoot.
- The child is uncomfortable wearing certain fabrics or having clothing tags touching their skin.
- The child does not enjoy cuddling or tickling.
- The child is easily startled by unexpected or loud noises.
- The child eats the same foods daily.
- The child sits awkwardly and fidgets.

Figure 5-3

Action Signs

As previously noted, many of the risk factors for depression in children are risk factors for anxiety as well, and the two conditions often co-occur. Thus, the action signs for depression found in chapter 4 are applicable to children experiencing anxiety as well. However, they should be carefully reviewed according to the child's unique formula.

Additional action signs for childhood anxiety include the following:

Parent anxiety: Anxiety disorders tend to run in families. Children frequently mimic the anxious behaviors of their parents, and children whose mothers suffer from both anxiety and depression are at high risk of developing the conditions (O'Connor 2020).

Behavioral inhibition: Behavioral inhibition is the consistent tendency to show marked behavioral restraint or fearfulness with unfamiliar people, situations, or events, and it contributes to the early development of anxiety and depression in children.

High levels of behavioral inhibition have also been linked to increased risk of social phobias (Pahl et al. 2012).

Social challenges and withdrawal: Children who are experiencing anxiety can display uncontrolled impulsivity and social immaturity—for example, being excessively silly or chattering nervously—which poses social challenges. Social withdrawal, or choosing to minimize contact with others, is a common sign of anxiety. Its underlying causes and explanations vary from child to child. However, underlying reasons include poor self-esteem and social skills.

Peer victimization: Children who are bullied commonly experience anxiety. Without intervention, this can lead to poor concentration, social withdrawal, and a decrease in self-esteem.

Adverse childhood experiences (ACEs): Children who have a predisposition toward overarousal and hypersensitivity to stimuli due to ACEs are inclined to develop anxiety. Children who live in low-income families or whose parents are divorced, for example, are at a greater risk of developing anxiety. Parental conflict, stress, and lack of social support and resources significantly influence a child's predisposition to anxiety. For more information on ACEs, see chapter 2.

Controlling and overprotective parenting styles: Childhood anxiety commonly stems from feelings of having little control over life circumstances. Overprotective and intrusive parenting is linked to child social anxiety, including parental control displayed through unnecessary assistance, engaging in infantile behaviors, or invading a child's privacy.

Poor nutrition: Children whose nutritional needs are not properly met are at greater risk of mental and emotional challenges than children who receive appropriate daily nutrition. When a child's diet is deficient, anxiety can occur. For example, omega-3 fatty acids are inversely correlated with anxiety disorders (O'Neil et al. 2014).

Sensory processing issues: Children with sensory processing difficulties are prone to anxiety. Sensory challenges, such as crowds or certain clothing, make them feel overwhelmed about situations that trigger their sensitivities. Chapter 8 discusses the different sensory patterns of children. Figure 5-3 presents sensory issues that commonly accompany childhood anxiety.

◆◆◆◆◆

Like depression, children of all ages can suffer from anxiety and its long-term consequences. While contemplating strategies to support a child such as Jessica in overcoming anxiety, remember that many factors interact in complex ways to determine whether a strategy will be successful for the child—hence the significance of factoring in all the child's unique needs. Jessica presents with sleep difficulties, anger, and poor social skills, all of which require time and attention. Also deserving emphasis for Jessica is learning to trust that she will be safe when her mother drops her off at school every morning. A transitional object could help tremendously in grounding Jessica to the present, an important aspect of EIIPS for children experiencing anxiety.

As is true for childhood depression, creative pathways, such as beading and nature projects, are significantly helpful strategies that act as a portal into a child's anxious inner world. Part 2 of this book is devoted to practical strategies such as these for alleviating a variety of internalizing behaviors. Because research demonstrates that medication is not always the most effective option for supporting children who struggle with anxiety, EIIPS using creative pathways and parent-child interactions are recommended and, in most instances, most effective. When stakeholders learn how to successfully respond to a child's needs based on their unique formula, not only is a better relationship kindled, but trust is built and the stress that often propels a child's anxiety decreases or disappears.

Part II

Alleviating Internalizing Behaviors through Play

During play, interactions with musical instruments and other conduits for creativity are valuable in alleviating internalizing behaviors.

6

The Cathartic Powers of Play

Play is so integral to childhood that a child who does not have the opportunities to play is cut off from a major portion of childhood.

—Caroline Ramsey Musselwhite

Play is so important to optimal child development that it has been recognized by the United Nations High Commission for Human Rights as a right of every child (Milteer et al. 2012). Daily diverse playtime provides children a forum in which to face challenges, soothe anxiety, lift depression, overcome trauma, and learn to concentrate and regulate emotions. According to Sigmund Freud's *Psychodynamic Theory of Play* (see pages 28–29), children experiencing internalizing behaviors benefit from various forms of play and plenty of uninterrupted time for it within beautiful spaces. Freud also believed children require an abundance of diverse and creative tools to experience play's cathartic powers.

Children's play patterns represent their language; through play processes, they communicate and heal their inner worlds. It is one of the best communication tools for any child, but for children who have endured ACEs, play represents an especially valuable lifeline through which they can face fears and learn to cope with them. EIIPS are most effective when they use integrated and diverse play to meet the needs of children according to their unique formulas and to reap the benefits of play's cathartic powers. To this end, it is recommended that stakeholders create individually tailored prescriptive tool kits for children experiencing internalizing behaviors.

A Prescriptive Tool Kit

The term *prescriptive* is grounded in the work of Friedrich Froebel (1782–1852), who originated the concept of kindergarten and saw play as an important component in a child's development. Froebel insisted that children follow specific and prescribed guidelines within play yet have freedom within those parameters. "When freedom is provided within structure, children feel encouraged to explore strategies, and this helps children develop confidence and self-efficacy which leads to healthy outcomes including reduction of anxiety and inculcation of more positive behaviors," he wrote (Froebel 1887).

A prescriptive approach to play considers a child's unique formula and focuses on matching the cathartic powers of play to his or her specific challenges and needs. Creativity and flexibility are crucial components of a successful prescriptive tool kit. Like recognizing a child's unique formula, filling a prescriptive tool kit supports children experiencing internalizing behaviors and is a reflective and developmentally appropriate practice: the more the tool kit and its diverse play tools are personalized to the child, the more effectively the condition can be addressed.

It is important to remember that not only is a child's formula unique, but their individual circumstances are as well. Research reveals that adapted and personal interventions using play are successful in supporting childhood internalizing behaviors (Yogman et al. 2018). When children's emotional issues are identified and personally addressed as early as possible, their feelings and behaviors improve, thereby improving their relationships and development.

Adaptive Play Tools

The best materials for children to play with are open-ended and mobile, encourage creative thinking, and have no directions. They can be moved, carried, combined, torn apart, and put back together in multiple ways. Ultimately, the child decides how to use the materials. For children to invite, sustain, prolong, and reap the benefits of play's catharsis, they must be provided with the right tools. Adaptive play tools are tailor-made, such as mud, blocks, music, and movement. Adaptive play tools are meant to help children identify their thoughts and feelings and appropriately manage them. They are pathways by which children express their inner world and the meaning they have constructed of it.

A key factor in identifying adaptive play tools is considering the *whole* child. An internalizing behavior attacks a child's total being and causes considerable distress to a child's entire development. It zaps energy and motivation; steals confidence and joy; manifests anger and doubt; crushes the spirit; impedes learning; and causes sadness, low self-worth, and isolation. Consider a child with a chronic illness: whether physical or psychological in nature, it influences the child's psychosocial functioning. Such a child may become very lonely due to their condition, doubt their worth, become reluctant to participate in social activities, and even withdraw from peers altogether.

To adaptively and prescriptively support the child, the emphasis must be on discovering and using customized tools that focus on the child's whole developmental makeup and cultural being. In providing these tools as pathways to creativity and self-expression, early childhood professionals take on new roles as child formula specialists, striving to support the early identification, prevention, and intervention of internalizing behaviors.

Twenty-Five Cathartic Powers of Play

Children are exposed to more family crises and trauma nowadays than in earlier generations (Masten 2018; Zarei 2020). Such adversity places tremendous stress on their developing systems and can lead to anxiety, depression, and social withdrawal. There has been considerable research on the impact of such childhood stress on children's development; adverse childhood experiences (ACEs) are discussed in depth on pages 32–34. Dr. William Stixrud explains, "Stress hormones actually turn off parts of the brain that allow [children] to focus attention, understand ideas, commit information to memory and reason critically" (Pica 2015, 17). With this in mind, as well as the speed and complexity of children's development, those entrusted with their care should have a working knowledge of play's cathartic potential to combat emotional wounds and developmental delays caused by ACEs.

The integration of the natural world into this book's framework and working definition of play is based on the naturally occurring restorative and healing elements of the outdoors, such as fresh air and sunshine. Natural outdoor play spaces also provide children with opportunities for choice, challenge, and risk, all reasons that play in the natural world should be an integral part of a child's curriculum—especially if they struggle with emotional turmoil. Chapter 9 is devoted entirely to the cathartic power of play in the natural world and how it acts as a means for a cure.

As mentioned, play—particularly play incorporating nature, creativity, and a child's senses—enables effective catharsis to disclose the underlying emotional issues that often impede a child's development. What follow here are twenty-five specific powers of play and their usefulness to children struggling with internalizing behaviors, all of which will guide the information outlined in the rest of part 2.

The Cathartic Powers of Play	
1. Play allows self-expression.	14. Play strengthens self-control.
2. Play teaches.	15. Play nurtures competence.
3. Play permits storytelling.	16. Play regulates emotions.
4. Play reenacts.	17. Play permits make-believe.
5. Play heals.	18. Play drives creativity.
6. Play accesses the unconscious.	19. Play empowers problem solving.
7. Play redirects.	20. Play encourages empathy.
8. Play transcends barriers.	21. Play is a rehearsal.
9. Play creates bonds.	22. Play accelerates development.
10. Play promotes resilience.	23. Play builds identity.
11. Play shapes values.	24. Play improves physical health.
12. Play relieves stress.	25. Play digests.
13. Play counteracts adverse emotions.	

Figure 6-1

1. Play allows self-expression. Friedrich Froebel stated, "Play is the highest expression of human development in childhood, for it alone is the free expression of what is in a child's soul" (Froebel 1887). Due to their limited vocabulary and inability to think abstractly, young children tend to struggle to express their thoughts and feelings verbally—especially emotions connected to unsettling memories and experiences. Play lets them comfortably express themselves through symbols such as puppets and dolls.

2. Play teaches. Research suggests that play is a key ingredient in learning. It teaches children how to socialize, think, solve problems, and mature through trial and error, exploration, experimentation, and collaboration. Children can learn emotional coping skills or academic concepts through play because it is, by definition, intrinsically motivated. For example, manners can be taught at a tea party. Play also propels a child's language development and intrinsic motivation and builds science, technology, engineering, arts, and math (STEAM) skills, such as sorting and classifying.

3. Play permits storytelling. Because storytelling crosses cultural borders, children from all over the world can learn valuable principles when play is coupled with a story. An illustration is *Aesop's Fables*—classic stories that teach children important lessons. Play soaked in storytelling helps children create narratives of their own lives and imitate those of others. They learn from characters, connect their lives to the story, and consider what they would do if they were in the characters' shoes. Observing children involved in different forms of play can also convey useful "stories" about children's inner worlds and family dynamics to caregivers. The patterns, sequences, sounds, and facial expressions a child uses during play speak volumes.

4. Play reenacts. Through play, children can practice "repetition compulsion," in which they symbolically reenact, change, embellish, and repeat stressful experiences until they understand and achieve emotional mastery over them. Such reenactment stimulates catharsis and allows a child to regain a sense of control over their world (Powers 2018; Reis 2019). In "The Therapeutic Powers of Play and Play Therapy," Schaefer and Drewes (2011) write that following 9/11, when children erected block towers and crashed small objects into them, they were processing the horrors they experienced that day (6).

5. Play heals. Erik Erikson emphasized that "to play it out is the most natural self-healing measure childhood affords" (Erikson 1950, 222). Play allows children to heal from stressful feelings, experiences, and emotional pain. As they walk through and try to make sense of uncomfortable emotions, the catharsis allows children to heal as they process inner disturbances at their own pace using preferred play pathways of self-expression. For example, children who are tactile learners can free physical and emotional tension they have bottled up when they participate in active play at a sensory table manipulating chilled lavender-scented playdough with a heavy rolling pin.

6. Play accesses the unconscious. Freud saw play as a natural and effective means of accessing rich data residing in the unconscious. Play acts as a grounding device and, he wrote, "offers children a familiar, neutral base to disclose unconscious struggles using defense mechanisms like projection, displacement, and symbolization" (Schaefer and Drewes 2011, 6). Play allows a child to take an active role in taming painful emotions and self-deprecating impulses.

7. Play redirects. Freud used the term *transference* to describe how children can relearn maladaptive skills, redirect intrusive thought patterns, and transfer painful emotions onto objects. For example, using play, caregivers can redirect children to ask for what they want instead of aggressively grabbing something from another child's hands. Or suppressed anger in a child can be symbolically transferred onto a canvas—the child can paint to redirect painful feelings.

8. Play transcends barriers. Play transcends racial, cultural, social, physical, and economic barriers. When children of all temperaments and backgrounds play together, they are inevitably confronted with challenges. However, because children are born free of prejudices, their innate curiosity and need to belong, interact, and connect draw them together, sustain their playtime, and allow them to make connections with others who may not look or speak like them. When children play with others from different backgrounds, they develop important social skills, including tolerance and kindness.

9. Play creates bonds. Play connects children with their imagination, their environment, their family, and their world, helping them to build lasting bonds and become emotionally attached to their caregivers. Play helps children with attachment problems become more confident and social. Through playful activities, such as making messy mud cakes together, children socialize, share their feelings, and learn to enjoy the company of one another. When socially withdrawn children learn to play using appropriate social skills, their moods and relationships improve.

10. Play promotes resilience. Resilience is the capacity to get back in balance after being pushed out of it—to tolerate challenges without breaking down. A child's imagination sparked during play stimulates protective factors, such as self-regulation, which builds resiliency. Collaboration, problem solving, and conflict resolution also feed into resilience and are involved in children's play. Play helps prepare children for change, spring back from the unexpected, and become emotionally flexible. It supports children in adjusting to new settings and dealing with surprises. It promotes resilience because it gives children the ability to recover quickly from setbacks. Children who are resilient have significantly fewer social problems, more advanced development, and higher self-esteem.

11. Play shapes values. Play reveals cultural values and requires communication and cooperation among children as they try out different roles and follow selected rules. They experience the cause and effect of disagreements as they decide on their designated details of play. Values based on negotiation, compromise, empathy, and fairness begin to take shape. During play free from adult directives, children develop an understanding of morality as they self-govern, invent, and enforce rules. For example, they decide among themselves on what is fair and unfair, what behaviors are acceptable and unacceptable, and how unacceptable behaviors will be dealt with.

12. Play relieves stress. Play counters the toxicity of stress because of its intrinsic enjoyment, letting children tap into creative pathways to express themselves and to release worry. It gives children opportunities to share their fears and role-play coping strategies. It relieves emotional wariness and reduces fear, anxiety, stress, and irritability. Children benefit when playtime is varied—for example, playing cooperatively with others, quietly alone on the floor, and energetically outdoors. Children are naturally drawn to play and are less likely to be anxious or depressed when it is part of their day, because its pleasure acts as an emotional distraction, taking their minds off their fears and concerns. The more interesting and engaging the play is, the deeper the concentration and more intense the distraction.

13. Play counteracts adverse emotions. Play diametrically opposes a child's negative emotions. The term *reciprocal inhibition* explains how specific emotions are mutually exclusive (Wolpe 1958). For example, fear and relaxation cannot exist simultaneously. Likewise, laughter and play thwart and overcome sadness and anxiety. Consequently, children can conquer a fear of darkness, for example, by playing hide and seek at dusk. Play itself is a process that mitigates and counteracts anxiety, depression, and social isolation.

14. Play strengthens self-control. Children demonstrate their development of self-control when they can share a play tool or practice thoughtfulness by letting a peer take another turn. Children have minimal control over their lives, but during play they gain a sense of power and can suddenly oversee their desires. When deprived of play, a child's self-control fails to develop appropriately because they are unable to practice skills such as the give-and-take necessary for learning to understand others' emotions, words, and intentions; self-discipline to play successfully with others; and emotional regulation for impulse control. Play permits children to master these skills, positively reinforced and observed by caregivers.

15. Play nurtures competence. Rivkin (2014) emphasized that in an optimal play area, "children can safely experiment with taking risks, which helps them see themselves as powerful and competent" (6). Stuart Brown, author of "Play, Spirit, and Character" (2014), adds that play produces pleasure and joy, which lead children to the next stage of mastery. Through play, children can create and explore a conquerable world but one that challenges them—just enough—as they tinker and toy, fashion and form, compete and negotiate. When children master play missions and are successful within social circles, they gain a sense of competence and confidence. And for children who have endured significant stress, this sense of mastery is especially important, as it melts away feelings of powerlessness and highlights emotional control.

16. Play regulates emotions. Self-regulation is the ability to control emotions and behavior, resist impulses, and exert self-control. In my time as an educator, experience and observation has shown me that children's ability to regulate their emotions and control their impulses is one of the greatest indicators of school success. There is a direct relationship between play and social and self-regulatory skills. Children who have experienced considerable adversity often struggle to regulate their feelings and incoming sensory input; underlying tension and encoded sensations trapped in their bodies often drive internalizing behaviors such as anxiety and depression. Play teaches children how to self-regulate physiologically, an important first step in the healing process. Using play, they learn to regulate their bodies, their bodies' impulses, and their emotions and to anticipate consequences by thinking through their behaviors.

17. Play permits make-believe. When a child plays make-believe, language forms and lets the child create worlds where they can face fears, confront challenges, and be their own best self. Make-believe strengthens emotional muscles that allow children to step beyond their comfort zones. During make-believe play a child's dreams become a reality. For instance, a child who struggles with fear and anxiety can be the brave hero. A child who struggles with athletic pursuits can be an Olympic sprinter. A child's impulses and needs, many of which are typically blocked in real life, have a pathway to release through self-expression. Play permits children to enter fantasy worlds where they take on bigger, better, stronger, and more confident personal roles.

18. Play drives creativity. It is imperative to nurture a child's creativity using play. Creativity influences many aspects of a child's development, including problem solving and defeating emotional and social conflict. Play also provides children with opportunities to develop their imagination and process emotions in a nonthreatening and creative manner. Moreover, play and creativity are analogous, as literature, both past and present, confirms that the former increases the latter (Feitelson and Ross 1973; Lieberman 1965; Rose 2020). When children play, they focus on the means rather than the ends, sparking innovative strategies and out-of-the-box thinking as they step into powerful roles. For example, being king of a castle empowers a child who is withdrawn to take uncharacteristic risks and attempt creative solutions to challenges.

19. Play empowers problem solving. Play theorist Brian Sutton-Smith (2009) noted that during play, children develop the neurological foundations that allow language, abstract thinking, creativity, and problem solving. Through play, they learn specific as well as general information and mindsets toward problem solving that include abstraction and flexibility. Children must link together bits of random yet detailed information to form novel solutions to problems requiring the restructuring of thoughts, actions, and emotions. For example, during play children must problem solve social challenges regarding how to relate to others and how to regulate and move their bodies.

20. Play encourages empathy. Play develops a child's emotional intelligence and strengthens their ability to understand another's feelings and intentions, thus increasing their sense of empathy. When children play, especially when they role-play, they step into other worlds and begin to relate to their peers. They become more compassionate and more willing to share and take turns. Play in the natural world also teaches empathy and compassion for other living things.

21. Play is a rehearsal. Nearly everything a child needs to learn is developed and rehearsed in play. Within the context of play, children rehearse social competencies such as body language and learn to read others' emotions, cooperate, build friendships, and negotiate conflicts. When children play, especially when they engage in house play, they rehearse life skills by acting out roles and situations. For example, a child who is typically anxious and withdrawn can rehearse speaking up about their needs. Puppets are another way to rehearse skills. Through repeated rehearsal, play can transform a child's maladaptive body responses, thoughts, and feelings.

22. Play accelerates development. Play contributes to children's physical, social, and emotional well-being. It allows them to attempt new skills, experiences, and roles beyond their normal cognitive level. Children who are deprived of play often have developmental delays, poor emotional regulation, and underdeveloped language skills. Play permits the development of crucial cognitive functions, such as being aware of and controlling feelings and actions and the ability to organize, focus, plan, strategize, prioritize, and initiate. Ultimately, play accelerates the development of these abilities.

23. Play builds identity. Play gives a child the opportunity to discover their place in the world. The way children play reveals their interests, abilities, and fears; they develop their sense of self through play. It enables them to grapple with what they can and cannot do, their uniqueness, and their ability to think for themselves (Winnicott 1971). Play, regardless of form, allows children opportunities to self-reflect and consider "self in relation to others" (Mead 1934). Pretend play is particularly conducive to the development of self-talk. Cooperative play helps children learn how to find identity within a group. Explorative play provides children the opportunity to practice moving at their own pace and find endless ways to satisfy their curiosity. Play in the natural world is important to children's development of independence, allowing them to try out increasing distances from their caregiver.

24. Play improves physical health. Children play because it makes them feel good, and consequently, positive emotions promote long-term health. Daily physically active play accomplishes aerobic conditioning, which reduces stress. Laughter sparked during physical play also lessens stress, boosts moods, and stimulates children's immune systems. Physical play, especially outdoors, increases attention span, decreases hyperactivity, and improves the efficiency of thinking and problem solving.

25. Play digests. Every aspect of a child's life is affected by play and sets the stage for all subsequent development. Considering how all its mentioned cathartic powers and forms intertwine with a child's developmental stages, play is the natural medium for children to make sense of and digest their worlds. Like digestive enzymes work as a catalyst to break down food to enhance other systems of the body, play too takes on a comparatively supportive role. Ultimately, it affects every aspect of a child's physical, emotional, and sensory experience and absorbs them as developmentally needed for daily functioning. By way of these influences, play promotes mental health: "Restoring children's free play is not only the best gift we could give our children; it is also an essential gift if we want them to grow up to be psychologically healthy and emotionally competent adults" (Gray 2011, 459).

◆◆◆◆◆

The American Academy of Pediatrics (AAP) promotes a play prescription for the healthy development of children, particularly children struggling to regulate and process uncomfortable feelings. When children are engrossed in play and encouraged to work through its creative processes, its therapeutic capabilities are activated. Everything from snack time to transitioning and cleanup become opportunities for stakeholders to spark play power. By investing in a prescriptive tool kit grounded in play's cathartic powers, we maximize those powers. Of particular importance are adaptive play tools, which enhance and develop a child's whole play experience within the environment and across the curriculum. Through its many forms, play becomes a remarkably diverse and flexible means of communication, self-expression, and healing for children experiencing internalizing behaviors. The many forms of play and ways to diversify a child's play menu are outlined in the next chapter.

7

Integrating a Diverse Play Menu

The play's the thing
Wherein I'll catch the conscience of the king.

—William Shakespeare, Hamlet

Neophilia is a love of or enthusiasm for what is new or novel. Bob Hughes, author of *Evolutionary Playwork and Reflective Analytic Practice*, wrote, "Children are stimulated to play by the new, the novel, the attractive and the interesting. . . . [They] create their own neophilic context using imagination and fantasy" (quoted in Wilson 2010, 19). Many great American innovators have credited long days full of childhood play as sparking their most creative and novel ideas. For example, as boys, Wilbur Wright (1867–1912) and Orville Wright (1871–1948) were enthusiastic tinkerers who thrived and engrossed themselves in play—play that eventually acted as a catalyst for their innovative thinking, designing and building the world's first successful airplane (National Geographic Society n.d.).

As already mentioned, play's cathartic role in establishing strong mental wellness for a child is significant. Play is a child's natural way to redirect uncomfortable feelings and recreate overwhelmingly painful and adverse experiences. For example, child Holocaust survivors recalled play as having been a sustaining and surviving force amid deplorable concentration camp conditions. George Eisen (1988) shared, "Play [was] a subset of life in which one [could] rehearse for the serious business of adaption . . . in a play setting. But in the same context, play . . . create[s] an arrangement in which a child can practice behavior eminently directed for survival" (11). Countless studies, surviving documents, detailed memoirs, and diaries, dating back decades, recognize and draw on the proven therapeutic power of play on a child's development.

This chapter discusses several forms of play, how each form serves a child's development, and how tapping into children's interests to create more meaningful play experiences is essential for establishing sound mental wellness. Outdoor play, in which children can more readily experience the cathartic value of nature and its healing elements, is also discussed and greatly encouraged. (Chapter 9 is devoted to outdoor play.) My hope is that the content will act as a springboard for the development of other imaginative techniques to fill prescriptive tool kits. Not every approach will work for every child, but offering a diverse play menu will better allow a child to meet the needs of their unique formula.

Physical Play

The positive influence of physical play on a child's development is evident in the research literature. Researchers from the Institute of Medicine claim that children who are active pay attention better and have faster cognitive processing speed. Physical play—any activity that involves the body's large muscles or the use of the whole body—is effective in addressing internalizing behaviors, as it helps children process emotional stress caused by adverse childhood experiences (ACEs) and supports social skills rehearsal. Regularly scheduled physical play benefits a child's development in many ways, including those outlined in figure 7-2. Physical play also naturally teaches children self-soothing techniques such as relaxed breathing. When children fail to participate in consistent physical play, they become more susceptible to preventable health conditions. The American Academy of Pediatrics (AAP) recommends at least sixty minutes of daily physical activity for preschool-aged children (Pellegrini and Bohn-Gettler 2013).

Furthermore, children can focus better when allowed physical play using creative movement breaks throughout the day to move and stretch their bodies. When introducing creative movements to children, it is helpful to physically demonstrate the activities with clear verbal explanations. Use and actively model key verbs, adverbs, and

Suggestions to Integrate a Child's Play Menu

- Incorporate literacy and language props into play spaces:
  - menus
  - old rotary telephones
  - memo pads
  - envelopes
  - books (address, phone, cooking, appointment)
  - mini whiteboards
  - old calendars
  - junk mail
  - greeting cards
  - grocery coupons and ads
  - eye charts
  - open/closed signs
  - stationery
  - clipboards
  - writing utensils
- Offer assorted clothing, shoes, and accessories:
  - purses and briefcases
  - scarves, capes, and hats
  - costume jewelry and boas
  - bow ties and suspenders
- Use assorted clothing from different cultures and professions:
  - tutus
  - kilts
  - helmets
  - saris
  - aprons and chef's hats
- Offer various textures:
  - suede
  - corduroy
  - leather
- Provide small, unbreakable hand mirrors or a full-length mirror for dress-up play.
- Change up play furnishings and extend play area boundaries as much as possible to keep children interested. For example, with a few prop changes, a puppet theater can be converted into an old-fashioned general store or drive-in restaurant.
- Seek out donated uniforms from charity shops or restaurants.
- Define play boundaries with walls, shelves, and furniture to create a temporary secluded area.
- Create separate spaces, such as a kitchen and living room. Within play spaces, offer tools that are not usually used together, such as tennis rackets and small beanbags.
- Group or pair children during play to provide opportunities for children to learn from each other in complementary ways. Allow children to showcase strengths and support weaknesses with sensory play.
- Consider the following: outside, lay out three or four tires and fill each with different nature-oriented, sensory material. For example:
  - Fill one tire with sand and sand tools.
  - Fill the second tire with small containers of nature items such as acorns, small nuts, seedpods, and shells for making jewelry.
  - Fill the third tire with mud and containers for making mud pies.

Figure 7-1

prepositions. For example, when children hear and perform "walk slowly" or "gallop quickly," they learn the meanings of words to more accurately express themselves in social situations. When children move *over* a log, *under* a table, *around* a tree, *through* a tunnel, *across* the monkey bars, and *along* the balance beam, these abstract words take on concrete meaning. When children perform action words such as *stomp*, *pounce*, *stalk*, and *slither*, they understand how their bodies can perform the motions.

Benefits of Physical Play

- Physical play naturally relaxes, soothes, and helps children release bottled-up energy and stress.
- Physical play reduces anxiety, helps children focus and stay alert, and improves their mood.
- Physical play increases a child's attention span, which helps them sustain learning and playing, which increases a child's self-confidence.
- Physical play helps children maintain proper body weight and improves their overall health.
- Physical play supports children in developing important socialization skills and impulse control.
- Physical play helps children become aware of their bodies and how they function.

Figure 7-2

Fantasy Play

Children have a proclivity for fantasy play, also known as imaginative play, creative play, pretend play, make-believe, and dramatic play. Fantasy play is considered one of the most effective therapeutic tools for children to process strong feelings and express their thoughts. It not only offers them an outlet for emotional release but also encourages listening skills, boosts problem solving, and allows assertiveness, creativity, and compromise. Fantasy play also allows children to strengthen their identity by giving them a sense of power and mastery that is not possible in their real world, resulting in increased emotional regulation and positive feelings.

This form of play consists of verbal expression, body language, improvisation, and role play. It gives children the power to step into a world of make-believe and explore themes that interest them. Fantasy playtime is especially important for children experiencing internalizing behaviors and offers countless benefits for those struggling

Please consider . . .
The Bumblebee Waggle

Send a newsletter home to families that shares ideas to promote physical play and encourages children to fully engage their imaginations in place of sedentary activities, such as watching television. Suggest childhood favorites such as Follow the Leader or creative multicultural, multisensory, and cross-curriculum movement activities such as The Bumblebee Waggle.

According to entomologist James Danoff-Burg, "the waggle dance is used by bees to communicate to other bees back at the hive the distance, direction, and the quality of food they have found" (2002, 46). Discuss this bumblebee behavior with children. Encourage them to pretend to fly in a swarm, gather nectar from flowers, and carry it back to a hive. Play the orchestral work "Flight of the Bumblebee" by Nikolai Rimsky-Korsakov while the children "fly." Make homemade bee wings as creative props and attach them to the children's backs.

Or try the Make Me a Machine game. Ask children to list as many machines as they can think of. To get them started, mention washing machines, vacuum cleaners, microwaves, computers, remote controls, telephones, and radios. Show them pictures of various machines and explain that machines help us in diverse ways. Next, challenge the children to make themselves into machines. Encourage them to twist and turn like beach towels in a washing machine, jump about like popcorn popping in a microwave, and so on. Demonstrate noises such as *boing*, *ping*, *whoosh*, *beep*, *honk*, and *shhh*.

For additional creative movement break ideas, refer to the chart on page 159.

with symptoms. Moreover, children experience tremendous satisfaction from both the process and the product of fantasy play, which generally takes one of the forms listed in the figure that follows. Each form should be integrated into a child's environment.

Benefits of Fantasy Play
◆ Fantasy play offers a child an outlet for emotional release. ◆ Fantasy play promotes listening skills. ◆ Fantasy play encourages creativity and compromise. ◆ Fantasy play promotes assertiveness. ◆ Fantasy play uses abstract and representational thinking. ◆ Fantasy play deeply nurtures social skills.

Figure 7-3

Fantasy Play Form	Benefit to a Child's Development
House play	◆ When children play house or use dollhouses to play, they learn to do a variety of things: • compromise • negotiate • socialize • cooperate • engage in fine-motor skills (such as folding towels, brushing a doll's hair, or fastening clothes) ◆ Children often mimic their life experiences while playing house or using dollhouses. ◆ The house that a child creates frequently reveals a significant amount about their emotional state and family identity that can be traced to ACEs. ◆ Stakeholders can learn a lot about children's mental wellness and home life from observing their house play or play with dollhouses.
Dress-up play	◆ Role-playing through dress-up allows children to try out alternative behaviors to confusing situations. ◆ Dressing up in creative, cultural, and festive costumes is a proven therapeutic method for children with internalizing behaviors to play out hurtful feelings and traumatizing situations through make-believe. ◆ Explain to children (and concerned caregivers) that dressing up is an activity for any gender. ◆ Children dressing up as a gender different from their own is common and a part of healthy development.

Themed fantasy play	◆ A child's obsession with a specific theme often signals deeper unresolved issues or inner conflicts. For example, if a child's pet dies, the child may become preoccupied with death. ◆ Children typically try to deal with conflict and its associated thoughts and emotions with themed play. ◆ Using themed play, their defenses relax, but often anxiety, fear, sadness, and confusion surface. ◆ With diverse themed play, children can bring to life subjects that interest and worry them or venture to worlds never explored. ◆ Environments should offer new themes regularly and use props that represent both magical and far-off worlds and real settings. ◆ Offer practical and relevant play tools, such as these: • baby dolls with bottles • cars and emergency vehicles • actual bandages in a doctor's kit • illustrated books to accompany themes

Figure 7-4

Please consider . . . Using Two Dollhouses

Consider making two dollhouses with dolls of a range of sizes and roles available in a child's play environment. Erikson (1950) noted that the playhouse is the only repeatedly occurring play symbol that emphasizes how children often view themselves and their world. Many traumatic events that children face rationalize the use of two dollhouses:

- A change in a child's family structure, such as divorce or separation (one weekend spent at Mom's house and the next weekend at Dad's house)
- The birth of a new sibling
- Moving through numerous foster care placements without ever working through the initial trauma of the separation process
- Conflict with friends, neighbors, or relatives

Ideas for Fantasy Play Themes

- Castle with a moat and drawbridge
- Art studio or bakery
- Barbershop or beauty shop
- Circus
- Dentist, veterinarian, or doctor's office
- Marketplace
- Post office
- Schoolhouse
- Five-star restaurant
- General store or old-time mercantile

Figure 7-5

Please consider . . .
The Effectiveness of Fantasy Play

Fantasy play is most effective for children between the ages of three and five. Please consider the following points about fantasy play:

- According to Erikson's *Theory of Psychosocial Development* (see page 29), children's development is established and molded in the *initiative* stage when they are given numerous opportunities to participate in fantasy play, as it sparks creativity.
- When children are forced to forgo the *initiative* stage and prematurely pushed into the next stage, called *industry*, valuable growth, spontaneity, and imagination are lost.
- It is vital for stakeholders to realize that a child's ability to identify, regulate, and sort out their emotions and thoughts is a major aspect of mental wellness that requires a process.
- Children must experience each developmental stage because each stage has a direct effect on the other.

Cooperative Play

Cooperative play, when children actively play together, has many benefits, which are summarized in figure 7-6. Cooperative play helps children develop socially and emotionally; promotes self-control; and increases self-esteem, motivation, compassion, and tolerance of others' similarities and differences. It is especially useful for children with internalizing behaviors, who often struggle to socialize and make friends. Play involving group games, tasks, and play projects is valuable for promoting positive peer interactions.

In this section, the focus will be on cooperative play using projects to promote positive peer interactions with all sorts of child temperaments. This type of play involves a small group of children working toward a common goal to which each child must contribute. A cooperative project is ideal for children experiencing internalizing behaviors for several reasons: it gives them a sense of community and accomplishment when the task is complete, it requires them to work in incremental stages, and it teaches them to use trial and error and socialization to successfully complete the project. Children must also demonstrate success at each stage to move on to the next one, which keeps motivation high.

Additionally, cooperative play project work is a natural mode of learning for children. It allows them to practice responsibility through teamwork and can turn everyday experiences, such as chores, into powerful socializing opportunities. For example, children can use a living storybook project (listed in figure 7-7) to conclude a week-long storybook theme. Keep in mind that play spaces and projects are enhanced when children have access to diverse and relevant books on the topics.

Benefits of Cooperative Play

- Cooperative play strengthens relationships.
- Cooperative play improves children's decision-making skills.
- Cooperative play develops a child's language skills.
- Cooperative play fosters self-expression.
- Cooperative play improves social skills, such as learning to take turns.
- Cooperative play encourages empathy.

Figure 7-6

Long Cooperative Play Projects	
Fall leaves project	◆ Seasonal experiences in nature are crucial for healthy development. ◆ Children can work as a team to rake up autumn leaves. Provide child-sized rakes and leaf bags. ◆ Before the children bag up the leaves, let them safely jump into a few leaf piles.
Living storybook project	◆ Encourage children to bring a storybook to life through skits and plays. ◆ Let them choose the book, assign the roles, create the costumes, and make the scenery and props. ◆ Invite families and other classes to the children's final presentations.
Scavenger hunt	◆ During an indoor or outdoor hunt, have children carry a small bag, pad of paper, and pencil as they search for clues. ◆ Leave simple laminated hints for children to follow throughout the environment. For example: • Find something blue. • Find a piece of trash. Put it in its proper place. • Find a bird's nest and a flower. Draw them.
Shoe polishing project	◆ Explore and chart jobs related to shoes. ◆ Research how shoes from all over the world are designed, made, repaired, sold, and polished. ◆ Demonstrate how to polish a pair of tap shoes and let children polish shoes using various brushes. ◆ Send a newsletter home to families asking for donations of shoes for children to polish.

Figure 7-7

Short Cooperative Play Projects

- Sweeping and cleaning up the playground with push brooms
- Shoveling snow or slush to clear paths with child-sized shovels
- Cleaning classroom furniture with sponges and soapy water
- Baking biscuits or scones with students; pounding out dough and cutting shapes
- Making apple cider from apples picked on a field trip to an orchard
- Shucking corn or shelling peas grown in a class garden
- Picking up litter from the playground together
- Planting flowers around the schoolyard

Figure 7-8

Constructive Play

Constructive play is the creative manipulation of materials to make things. For example, using blocks to build a tower is a simple form of constructive play. This form of play can be independent or cooperative, simple or complex. It is a critical mode of learning for a child's social, emotional, and cognitive development. When children can explore freely amid an assortment of creative materials, their play evolves. They better understand concepts when they can tinker and toy, assemble, invent, and build things for themselves.

Through constructive play, children can make anything if supplied enough materials, time, and support. Pages 192–193 offer a lengthy list of constructive play

Benefits of Constructive Play

- Constructive play encourages creativity.
- Constructive play encourages children to develop social skills and peer relationships.
- Constructive play inspires children to learn more about themselves and the world around them.
- Constructive play gives children opportunities to push their abilities and ideas.
- Constructive play promotes critical thinking.

Figure 7-9

materials. The possibilities for using these materials are endless; as you review the list, bear in mind that the materials can be used for other forms of play too. Please watch children closely at all times when they are playing with constructive materials.

Suggestions to Promote Constructive Play

- **Make constructive play tools portable.** For example, turn an old tackle box into a tote box for carrying tools from an indoor play area to one that is outdoors.
- **Establish clear and simple behavior expectations and procedures for constructive play.** For instance, blocks are never thrown.
- **Always have ample supplies of constructive play tools.** If there aren't enough, children may argue over them. Remember that miniatures from a fantasy play area—such as dollhouse furniture or people and animal figures—can be used for constructive play.
- **Incorporate blueprints in constructive play.** For example, someone creates a block tower, and then children recreate it using a blueprint. Or see who can build the tallest tower. Have children use tape measures to measure their creations.

Figure 7-10

Quiet Play

Quiet play, also known as solitary play, is a valuable way to access information about a child's feelings and the experiences that produced them. It offers rich cathartic value for children experiencing stress, helping them make connections to their experiences and granting them time to sort through their ideas and emotions, often putting the pieces together into a larger, more meaningful picture. Quiet play provides an escape from routine and offers a just-for-me refuge when children become overwhelmed. It is a useful mode when children struggling with internalizing behaviors have difficulty concentrating or interacting with peers or when they require privacy.

Beautifully designed quiet play spaces can provide a safe refuge for children with internalizing behavior symptoms, such as anxiety, by allowing them to refocus their energy, regain self-control, and relax. Never use a quiet play area as a time-out or punishment area. Also, while a quiet play area should be out of the way, it should never be completely hidden—make sure play areas can always be seen. Solitary, quiet play is important for all age groups to engage in, but it should never be a child's only form of play. Figure 7-11 presents the benefits of quiet play for children. Figure 7-12 offers ideas for incorporating quiet play into a child's environment.

Please consider . . . Using a Variety of Blocks

Blocks are favored constructive play tools. The following list offers ideas to make ordinary block play extraordinary and considers children's unique formulas:

- Offer a wide variety of blocks, such as large, hollow blocks, prism blocks, jumbo blocks, textured blocks, foam blocks, soft picture blocks, pattern blocks, wooden blocks, homemade blocks, unit blocks, and cardboard blocks.
- Orient block play to math and science by encouraging children to count, match, sort, and classify blocks. As children build with blocks, they grapple with gravity and balance and learn about shapes.
- Encourage literacy through block play. After children erect towers or bridges, let them make signs naming their creations or draw and write stories about them.
- Keep clipboards and art tools handy in a block play area.
- Offer tape or laminated strips to serve as roads. These supplies will help children exercise their imaginations and extend their block play.
- Hang posters of famous and beautiful structures to serve as inspiration, such as the Great Pyramid of Giza, the Parthenon, Notre Dame de Paris, the Leaning Tower of Pisa, the Taj Mahal, or the Great Wall of China.

Benefits of Quiet Play

- Quiet play allows children the opportunity to reflect and retreat from a busy day.
- Quiet play in beautifully prepared spaces makes children feel secure.
- Quiet play places stocked with books encourage literacy.
- Quiet play allows children who are feeling tired or out of control a place to regroup.
- Quiet play encourages development of individual cognitive skills.
- Quiet play fosters independence and self-confidence.

Figure 7-11

Suggestions for Promoting Quiet Play

- Encourage journaling or drawing in quiet play areas.
- Stock spaces with various tools, including the following:
  - markers, crayons, and pens
  - different writing surfaces, such as miniature blackboard slates, whiteboards, and clipboards
  - stamp pads, envelopes, and miscellaneous stickers
- Be willing to label drawings or write down stories for children.
- Set up a quiet corner for children under tables, behind furniture, and up in lofts.
- Use small mattresses and futons. Bunk beds make model lofts.
- Inundate quiet spaces with softness, from plush pillows and carpet squares to hammocks and beanbags in various shapes and sizes.
- Add puzzles, books, and other reflective activities for children.
- Make individual listening a part of children's quiet playtime.
  - Provide a CD or music player with headphones. Offer varied musical recordings or audio storybooks in a side basket.
  - Add stuffed animals to match themes from the listening selections.
- Water play is a great quiet activity for children experiencing internalizing behaviors. A water table, or any sensory table in a secluded area, allows children to experience the medium without distraction or interruption and to become engrossed in their thoughts.

Figure 7-12

In closing this chapter, it is beneficial to recall and review the power of play and its significance in children's mental wellness and development. A child's emotional state, cognitive abilities, and past experiences and memories merge to form a personal view of their world that they access during play. The types of play outlined in this chapter emphasize the importance of tapping into such play and its critical use as a child's natural means of self-expression, healing, and socializing. You have also seen how play can provide stakeholders valuable information about a child's emotional state, allow children to grow emotionally, and help them satisfy other developmental competencies, such as healthy emotional regulation.

Building on these central components of a child's mental wellness and development, the next chapter discusses how a child's environment plays a major role in the prevention of and intervention in internalizing behaviors and must be considered if ACEs are included in a child's unique formula. The next chapter details essential features of a child's environment for EIIPS and how the environment should incorporate these elements to allow the time, space, guidelines, and boundaries to practice, build, and master developmental building blocks.

8

Environmental Needs for Strong Mental Wellness

When a flower doesn't bloom, you fix the environment in which it grows, not the flower.

—Alexander Den Heijer, National Youth At-Risk Conference

As previously mentioned, in many cases, a child's problematic behavior is the result of an unmet normal, daily developmental need coupled with a playless environment, rather than an internalizing behavior. In 2018 the American Academy of Pediatrics (AAP) published "The Power of Play: A Pediatric Role in Enhancing the Development in Young Children," which outlines the benefits of play to "promote social-emotional, cognitive, language, and self-regulation skills that build executive function and a prosocial brain" (Yogman et al. 2018, 1). In the piece, the AAP also encourages prescribing play for children's healthy development, particularly children trying to manage toxic stress such as that from adverse childhood experiences (ACEs).

Whether children struggle with an internalizing behavior or not, they must feel secure in their environment to reach their full developmental potential. The environment must be set up to facilitate varied play, make children feel safe, and allow them to practice skills without repeated failure. The environment must be a place where children think, *It's all right for me to make a mistake. It's all right for me to choose my favorite color. I'm safe here because I matter.* It should encourage risk taking, build confidence, energize eager participation, and allow them to feel connected, valued, and successful. The environment's spaces and lessons should recognize their unique formulas while considering the key characteristics of child development covered in chapter 2.

Virginia Axline (1947) advised that a child's environment must be a "good growing ground," explaining it should provide the appropriate climate for children to experience themselves fully and to practice developmental skills. Maria Montessori (see pages 27–28) emphasized that the environment should be well prepared for play, and that when done so according to children's needs, it is possible for stakeholders to better understand children's mental and emotional functioning.

In chapter 7, we looked at how play and its varied forms influence a child's development and mental wellness. Additional factors that tremendously impact both are a child's environment and the relationships and interactions within it. Environment is so significant that it's considered nearly impossible for any of the other concepts discussed in this book to be effective unless the essentials of environmental support are provided. When a child's environment is carefully prepared, integrated with varied play, and personalized with essential elements, internalizing behaviors can be effectively addressed.

Remember that a young child's brain has a remarkable ability to adapt and change and is most flexible early in life to accommodate various environments, interactions, and changes. Yet creating such a setting is an ongoing process. As time passes, children develop, and their relationships and interactions with the world evolve. Children also respond differently to environments depending on their unique formulas. A child's temperament, culture, and developmental rate of language acquisition are other aspects to consider.

Additionally, children learn a great deal from each other—for example, how to share and take turns. Their curiosity and play within a thoughtfully prepared environment can produce positive energy. On the other hand, a poorly organized environment can stifle play and exacerbate internalizing behaviors. Regardless of how well an environment may work for one child, it will not work for every child, and a mismatch between a child's unique formula and the environment can cause behavioral and emotional challenges. For example, fluorescent lightning can distract some children, leading to poor attention and behavior.

Targeting Social and Emotional Milestones

The goal of this chapter is to guide you in creating an environment that integrates varied forms of play. It presents play strategies to effectively address internalizing behaviors by using play's cathartic function to target early childhood social and emotional developmental milestones. Children should be successfully displaying the social and emotional milestones outlined in figure 8-1 by age eight, which falls within the fourth stage of Erikson's *Theory of Psychosocial Development*, industry versus inferiority (page 30). Stakeholders should use figure 8-1 as a point of reference while observing children with concerning behaviors.

The strategies presented here encourage hands-on, active, sensory-driven play to stimulate a child's brain. They emphasize an environment where children can successfully play, interact, be supported with their emotional struggles, and advance in overcoming them. Thus, schedules and routines must be adjusted throughout the day to allow children to explore the environment uninterrupted. To accomplish these goals, the chapter discusses essential environmental needs for children and examples of how to integrate the varied play forms suggested in chapter 7 into the setting. Children's individual interests, unique formulas, and sensory issues are considered as well.

Characteristics of an Environment Supportive of Internalizing Behaviors

Children require a diverse and integrated environment that meets individual needs while being accessible to every child, regardless of ability. It's worth repeating: children differ in their abilities to process and respond to information from within their environment. For instance, Dori struggles to sit still during circle time, while Carly moves timidly when outdoors. They react in different ways because they absorb the environment's information differently in unison with not only their senses but other internal and external factors, such as what they had for breakfast or how much sleep they received the night before. But when a child constantly struggles to socialize and interact with peers, to maintain appropriate emotional regulation, or to appropriately participate in activities, stakeholders can use an understanding of the essential elements integrated into the environment to meet children's unique needs.

These elements are important for the healthy development of all children, but they are even more imperative for children struggling with internalizing behaviors. Identifying and catering to a child's unique formula and allowing various forms for self-directed free play creates a powerful environment for overcoming internalizing behaviors.

Early Childhood Social and Emotional Developmental Milestones (as developmentally age-appropriate and increasing in skill mastery)

- The child interacts with peers and shows an increase in ability to form friendships.
- The child participates in constructive play with one or more peers.
- The child initiates interactions with peers and adults.
- The child takes turns and shares materials appropriately.
- The child listens when others are speaking and interrupts less.
- The child participates in back-and-forth peer and adult conversations.
- The child helps problem solve with peers and seeks to resolve conflict.
- The child uses words, not inappropriate behaviors, to express emotions.
- The child demonstrates self-regulation of behaviors and emotions.
- The child joins peers in play, showing an increasing ability to socialize.
- The child can remain focused and persist with a task.
- The child can work and play both independently and cooperatively.
- The child increasingly shows impulse control.
- The child presents with an appropriate self-concept.
- The child is aware that personal actions have consequences.
- The child is aware of different emotions and responds to different emotions with increasing appropriateness.
- The child initiates communication to negotiate wants and needs.
- The child engages in fantasy play appropriately.
- The child identifies themselves as part of a family or class unit.
- The child seeks comfort when in emotional or social distress.

Figure 8-1

A child's successful interaction with the environment is greatly influenced by the essential needs listed in figure 8-2.

The Environment Allows Consistent, Creative Movement

Numerous studies demonstrate the power of movement on a child's learning processes, potential, behavior, and emotions (Pica 2015, 49). Research shows that a child's brain is considerably more active during movement than while stationary. As brain-based learning expert Eric Jensen puts it, "The brain is constantly responding to environmental input" (2006, 52). Or, in neurologist Carla Hannaford's words, "If you look at brain development, it's very, very clear that all areas of the brain are connected to the movement area. The very first areas of the brain are all directly around movement" (1995, 49).

There are countless simple strategies for incorporating movement into an environment meant to encourage not only movement but physical play, socialization, and self-expression—refer to page 184 for recommendations. These can be easily modified

Essential Environmental Needs to Support Internalizing Behaviors

- The environment allows consistent, creative movement.
- The environment stimulates each of a child's senses.
- The environment nurtures competence and security.
- The environment encourages family involvement.
- The environment cultivates independence and control.
- The environment implements organization and predictability.
- The environment provides choice.
- The environment effectively integrates play tools.
- The environment incorporates richness.
- The environment provides various integrated play spaces.
- The environment permits privacy.
- The environment offers creativity and self-expression.

Figure 8-2

and expanded upon to suit a child's individual and sensory needs. If a setting is too small to contain a movement area or activity, seek out a separate spot, such as an empty room, alcove, or hallway. Floor space used for movement areas and activities should be carpeted or padded appropriately. To increase the socialization potential within areas, provide music and props such as colorful scarves, crepe paper streamers, and ribbons. Also, please consider creative movement as a means of effectively transitioning children from one activity to the next. For additional movement suggestions, refer to page 184.

Handout 10: Creative Movement Ideas

www.redleafpress.org /tpp/h-10.pdf

Children are more primed for learning when they take periodic breaks for movement to stretch and get their wiggles out. This handout presents a variety of creative multicultural and multisensory ideas that are sharable in a newsletter sent home to families.

The Environment Stimulates Each of a Child's Senses

By incorporating sensory activities and materials, early childhood educators can enrich their classroom environments and, in turn, the learning experiences of young children. Montessori emphasized that stakeholders should pay attention to how an environment's sensory stimulation shapes a child's thinking because a child's behavior is predominantly driven by the way they define what they take in sensorially from the world. Too much stimulation can cause children to "turn off" their environment, while too little can send a child spiraling out of control trying to seek it out. During play, children fulfill their individual and optimal sensory arousal level. A child's environment should provide sensory stimulation to enhance individual development and include the use of their seven senses: *sight*, *sound*, *smell*, *taste*, *touch*, the *vestibular* sense (the body's sense of movement in relation to gravity), and *proprioception* (the body's sense of itself and its position in space).

Figure 8-3 provides examples of each sense, with ideas for incorporating them into children's daily activities and environment. The biggest thing to remember is that all of these treatment ideas are simply suggestions. Get creative using similar concepts. What works for one child may not necessarily work for another. Sensory play is all about trial and error.

Please consider . . .
Effective Transitioning

Children who struggle with internalizing behaviors often have difficulty transitioning from one activity to another and can become engrossed in their play, unable to switch gears without support. Smooth transitions in an environment prompt positive social behavior and help children experiencing internalizing behavior symptoms to be independent. For effective transitioning, physically model these actions for children:

- how to end an activity
- how to clean up
- how to move to the next activity
- how to gather materials
- how to ask for help if needed

Change can also be a source of considerable fear and anxiety for children who have experienced ACEs. One way to support children experiencing such anxiety is to use the same song or prompting to indicate a specific transition. Practice transitioning routines and add pizzazz to them. For example, use vibrant hand gestures or sing a song to transition. Sing songs in different languages.

Handout 11: Transitioning Ideas

www.redleafpress.org /tpp/h-11.pdf

In a child's environment, well-managed transitions provide opportunities for practicing concepts and skills. This handout offers suggestions to help structure transitions so they run smoothly and encourage learning.

Sensory stimulation influences how children regulate their emotions, attach meaning to their senses, and learn to react appropriately to both. For example, if a child becomes anxious due to loud noises, they can roll a squishy ball back and forth in their hands for support to calm down and self-regulate. Children with internalizing behaviors frequently struggle to handle feelings within their bodies and from their surroundings, such as sensitivity to temperatures, strong smells, and distracting background noise. While several frameworks exist for detecting and interpreting children's reactions to varied sensations, the way in which children integrate information from their environment is categorized into four processing styles: *low registering*, *sensory avoiding*, *sensory seeking*, and *sensory sensitive*. The environment is significantly expanded for a child when it builds on their interests, individualities, and sensory processing style.

You can implement a variety of techniques and tools throughout the day to help children comfortably experience their surroundings while integrating their senses according to individual needs and sensory issues. Regardless of strategy, please keep allergies and a child's personal needs in mind. For instance, never force a child to touch substances they describe as "yucky." Additionally, the following points are helpful to remember to maintain an environment that meets and expands children's personal needs:

- Recognize that strategies are not exhaustive, and what works for one child may not work for another.
- Consider sensory processing and its patterns.
- Understand all seven senses and how to meet them.
- Encourage healthy self-regulation using a child's senses and sensory needs.

These points are crucial within the context of chapters 1–5, as specific internalizing behaviors and their symptoms are presented.

Low-Registering Pattern

Children who are low registering require lots of motivating and display little interest in their surroundings. They seldom participate in activities, particularly during times of heavy commotion. Stakeholders can implement several simple strategies into the environment to help a child with a low-registering sensory pattern, including but not limited to the following:

- Remain near the child.
- Make eye contact when talking to the child and wait for a response after asking questions.
- Vary your voice level and facial expressions to help the child remain attentive.

Sight	Sound	Smell	Taste (Oral)
Add twinkling lights or miniature flashlights in a quiet area.	Play white noise, such as rain or ocean sounds.	Use vanilla and lavender fragrances; simmer potpourri.	Offer seltzer water.
Use contrasting colored displays.	Listen to a story with headphones while drawing a picture.	Write or color in a journal with scented markers.	Chew on sugar-free gum or licorice.
Practice letter formation in a sand or salt tray with colored paper at the bottom.	Provide musical instruments with various pitches, tones, and rhythms.	Help prepare snacks to experience smells.	Include textured foods at snack time, such as Jell-O and crackers.

Figure 8-3. Ideas to incorporate the seven senses into a child's routine. Adjust these to each child's unique sensory needs.

- Use cooperative play and group projects to encourage socializing.
- Provide activities and experiences that require movement.
- Have the child sit in the middle of activities, which offers more stimulation to help the child stay focused.

Sensory-Avoiding Pattern

Children who are sensory avoiding engage in behaviors to dodge overstimulation. Sensory-avoiding children require routine, and they struggle with transitioning, change, and new experiences. Stakeholders can implement several simple strategies into the environment to help a child with a sensory-avoiding pattern, including but not limited to the following:

- Monitor volume and pace of speaking.
- Avoid strong scents, such as perfumes, lotions, and room sprays.
- Help the child transition from one activity to the next.
- Offer short movement breaks to help with sensory overload.

Touch	Vestibular	Proprioception
Mix materials with contrasting feels, such as glitter and glue, sand and shaving cream, or paint and oatmeal.	Rock in a rocking chair or tire swing outdoors.	Push a loaded cart of books down the hallway.
Dress up in different-textured costumes with various fastenings.	Walk on a balance beam.	Squish playdough or a stress ball; cut heavy card stock paper.
Write letters in the air with a blindfold on or trace letters on a whiteboard with fingers.	Let children work in many positions, such as lying on the floor or sitting in a beanbag chair with a clipboard.	Have children try different movements: wheelbarrow walk, bear walk, crab walk, army crawl.

- Provide a quiet area the child can use when overstimulated.
- Discuss ways for the child to communicate distress or needs.
- Use verbal reinforcement for positive behavior, as sensory-avoiding children dislike being touched.
- Place the child at the end or beginning of lines for predictability.

Sensory-Seeking Pattern

Children who are sensory seeking fidget a lot, excite or overexcite easily, and actively seek out sensory experiences, including visual, auditory, tactile, and vestibular stimulation. Stakeholders can implement several simple strategies into the environment to help a child with a sensory-seeking pattern, including but not limited to the following:

- Give the child active jobs, such as shelving books.
- Let the child stand or sit on an exercise ball while working.
- Let the child use a fiddle object, such as a squishy ball or wad of playdough.
- Use lots of kinesthetic, hands-on activities.

- Let the child sit in the back of the room for lots of sensory stimulation (pace around, bounce on an exercise ball) and to decrease the chances of peers being distracted by their movements.
- Use consistent positive reinforcement and redirection.

Sensory-Sensitive Pattern

Children who are sensory sensitive are easily distracted by minor changes in their environment. They are easily startled by noises, visual stimuli, being touched, and movement around them. Children who are sensory sensitive protest things like a shirt tag touching their skin. Stakeholders can implement several simple strategies into the environment to help a child with a sensory-sensitive pattern, including but not limited to the following:

- Maintain a predictable schedule.
- Allow time and a private space for the child to go to when overwhelmed.
- Eliminate bright colors and an overabundance of distracting objects from walls.
- During cooperative play or group work, place the child with a small number of peers.
- Approach the child from the front to avoid startling them.
- Keep the environment as calm and organized as possible.
- Allow lots of choice making.

Handout 12: Instructional Strategies

www.redleafpress.org
/tpp/h-12.pdf

This handout presents creative and expressive instructional strategies to consider. Depending on the needs of the child, there are many ways a play or learning experience can be adapted.

The Environment Nurtures Competence and Security

Both Freud (1912) and Erikson (1950) highlighted children's intrinsic determination to be competent over developmental tasks and themselves within their environment. Erikson believed play enhances children's self-esteem because it naturally increases their sense of competence. An environment promoting competence engages children in high-quality exploration and discovery, supplies constant new sources of knowledge, and stimulates skill development and mastery. To feel capable, children must gain an inner sense of competence from their environment as they navigate their way through it. Children should also experience varied levels of success in the completion of everyday tasks. For example, a tightly closed glue bottle may cause initial frustration to a child but encourages problem solving and mastery of social skills, including asking for assistance.

Additionally, environments that promote competence foster security. Children experiencing internalizing behaviors require security and learn best in stimulating settings where they feel safe to play and explore spaces freely as well as interact with the people in them. Due to breaks they may have experienced in relationships where trust and security were needed, children with internalizing behaviors often struggle with tension, anxiety, and fear that impede the developmental processes needed to build nurturing relationships.

Poor relational bonding and nurturing can damage a child's feelings of wholeness, impulse control, and inner sense of security. A secure environment led by a trusting and caring teacher who promotes predictability, positive reinforcement, and open communication can repair such insecurities. In early childhood environments, relationship building between the teacher and child is crucial. Trusting, meaningful relationships evolve from the educator's ability to communicate understanding and security to and with a child.

Children typically develop emotional attachments through familiarity and comfort and are responsive to individuals who are sensitive to their needs. An environment promoting these features is led by a kind, trusting, and competent teacher whom children feel comfortable approaching throughout their day. Moreover, the warmth and comforting support of a trusted teacher influences a child's social and cognitive skills and encourages fewer behavior problems in the environment. Children who are not emotionally engaged by their teacher cannot grow intellectually.

An effective teacher nurtures children's unique formulas; guides, challenges, and comforts children; and uses developmentally appropriate activities and lessons. Quality educators model active listening, provide an outlet for expression of feelings, set limits, and are consistent in their daily practices because they know consistency promotes nurturing attachments and instills a sense of security in children with or without internalizing behaviors. Children are provided a safe, supportive environment where they can explore their developing competencies without being frustrated by unrealistic expectations placed on them by their teachers.

For more information on the importance of secure attachments, see pages 42–43.

The Environment Encourages Family Involvement

Guardian involvement in a child's world of play benefits both the child and the guardian because it establishes and strengthens bonds. Parent-child or guardian-child play opens doors for the sharing of values, increases communication, allows for teachable moments, and assists in problem solving. Playtime provides opportunities for the adult and child to confront and resolve individual differences and family-related concerns, and it allows the adult to view the world through the eyes of a child once again. Families are central to child development and should be an integral part of EIIPS. Not only do families play a critical role in the intervention of internalizing behaviors, but family involvement significantly reduces the likelihood of a child developing a condition in the first place. Involving families within the environment includes educating families about internalizing behaviors, symptomology, and resources for EIIPS, including definitions of a prescriptive play tool kit and tools within it. It's also important that families and stakeholders work closely and consistently as a team.

Family involvement can take many forms, including volunteering, participating in school activities, supporting children's play at home, and doing activities as a family, such as visiting the library or spending quality time together eating and exercising. Figure 8-4 provides additional ideas that promote family bonding. Recommended strategies include using community resources and programs such as library story time. Stakeholders can educate parents via weekly newsletters or webinars aimed at improving a child's dietary habits, sleeping, and screen time. Ultimately, family involvement should promote overall healthy development and mental wellness and intervene to prevent internalizing behaviors. Also noteworthy is that family involvement is synergistic: improvement in one area influences the quality of another. Chapter 1 outlines such suggestions and advises stakeholders to encourage families to use the information through consistent newsletters, educational material, and regular communication sent home.

Handout 13: The Importance of Family Involvement

www.redleafpress.org/tpp/h-13.pdf

Enthusiastically involve children and their families in activities that encourage communication, physical activity, affection, attention, and play. Suggestions are listed in this useful resource.

Strategies to Encourage Family Involvement

- Encourage families to praise their child's progress and efforts.
- Advise that families not refer to their child as depressed, anxious, or withdrawn, especially in front of the child.
- Discuss with families the importance of encouraging their children to interact with other children in environments outside of school, such as the park or church.
- Send home prosocial, behavioral, or emotional regulation books for families to read with their child. Refer to Handout 15: Literature to Develop Children's Social Skills.
- Remember that families face challenges such as poverty, addiction, and illiteracy that impact communication and involvement.
- Ask families to read up on their child's condition.
- Offer play resources and ideas for home.
- Suggest to families that they monitor their child's screen time and media use.
- Encourage families to engage in outdoor activities with their children.
- Discuss with families the importance of setting realistic goals for their child.
- Express that change and progress take time and consistency.
- Encourage families to help their children nurture a natural talent or an activity they feel passionate about, such as playing an instrument. Such nurturance helps develop self-confidence.
- Explain to families that continually scolding their child for depressed, anxious, or withdrawn behaviors or related conditions can be developmentally detrimental.
  - Use connection in place of correction. Connection may look like a warm embrace with encouraging words in a caring and calming tone.
  - View children's behavior as communication of their inner world. When inappropriate behavior surfaces, focus on what is driving it. If a child begins struggling to process "big" feelings, use connection to support the child in learning to self-regulate.
- Suggest predictability, consistency, and routines as much as possible because they increase a child's sense of security.
  - Recommend that families strive for regular bedtimes and mealtimes together.

Figure 8-4

The Environment Cultivates Independence and Control

Children need an environment that promotes individuality and autonomy where they can be in control of the content and intent of their play within prescribed parameters. Although cooperative play is important, children must also practice working independently. They must learn to sustain their efforts, press on when frustrated, and not depend solely on their teachers to stay on task—they must learn to think, negotiate, and problem solve for themselves. Because children gain a sense of independence through play, their environment should offer opportunities for individualized creative self-expression offered through various play spaces that encourage them to stay on task and work self-sufficiently for a specific time without excessive approval and support. As children develop skills and learn to regulate emotions, new play opportunities should become available to support their growth of competencies in these areas.

Children should also be allowed a sense of control in their environment, especially regarding the amount of individual sensory stimulation they take in from the setting. For example, consider Kyle. Kyle is working on his journal but finds it difficult to write amid the noise at his table. An environment promoting control allows Kyle the freedom to independently move to a quiet area to finish his work. Furthermore, giving children daily tasks, such as setting a table for snack time, passing out papers, or being the day's line leader, promotes independence and control over their environment and also ownership of it. As mentioned, an environment that offers children a diverse play menu where they have input over their sensory stimulation and what and how they play also endorses control. Well-defined boundaries in the environment also nurture independence and control.

Clear boundaries help lengthen children's playtime and enlarge their play ideas by setting defined limits on their freedom. Perhaps counterintuitively, boundaries encourage children to push themselves because they sense security within them. Clear boundaries also support effective environmental traffic flow and set limits. Clear and consistent boundaries help children focus, reduce disruptive behavior, and promote sustained play. Stakeholders can establish boundaries in many ways, including taped flooring, different-sized area rugs, strategically placed bookshelves, draped shower curtains, paneling, grab bars, carpet lines, storage units, furnishings, raised platforms, gazebos, canopies, boxes, or risers. Color is also a powerful visual organizer: children will quickly and easily learn to respond to a room with a yellow space for quiet play, a red space for fantasy play, or an orange space for block play. (For more on color, see the sidebar on page 115.)

Moreover, well-defined boundaries should be extended to a child's outdoor environment. Thickly vegetated spots can be used to define natural spaces to provide children with play opportunities such as hide-and-seek. Hedges, thickets, trees, and shrubs can also add corners and define borders or make hiding spots that allow children to

Please consider . . .
The Impact of Color in the Environment

Color can have a powerful influence on a child. The colors used in an environment can be calming or exciting, especially for children struggling to regulate their emotions and environmental sensory input. Carefully consider child sensitivities when deciding what colors to use for decorations, wall displays, bulletin boards, and whiteboards. Color selection extends to plant selection as well—use a variety indoors and outdoors. In the natural setting especially, consider flowers and foliage and how a plant responds to natural elements such as wind and rain.

Keep the following effects of color in mind:

- Light blue, soft violet, and green elicit comfort, relaxation, and security, making these shades suitable for quiet play areas.
- Yellow prompts children to feel happy and cheerful and is useful in art and music play spaces.
- Purple is best used as an accent color on bulletin boards and playground equipment.
- Warmer colors, such as orange and red, are more appropriate for movement or recreation play spaces.
- Use bright colors selectively on neutral-colored walls or shelves to highlight interest areas and mark storage spaces.
- Avoid covering entire walls with aggressive colors, such as bold reds, dark browns, or deep purples. At the same time, be mindful that completely white rooms look institutional.

observe wildlife with binoculars. Well-defined outdoor boundaries can also be created with natural sunken spots or surrounding slopes that give off a sense of enclosure. A bridge can serve as an outdoor boundary. Adding a floor to an outdoor play area with a pallet is another idea. Retaining walls can define the shape of a play area or section off zones for different purposes. For instance, use a retaining wall to section off an active play area from a class garden.

The Environment Implements Organization and Predictability

Children are naturally attracted to beautiful, well-organized places that are structured and predictable, with established routines. For children who struggle with internalizing behaviors, providing more structure to their routine is an effective way to increase their sense of security. Children often evaluate their surroundings with the question "What can I do here?" A child's environment should be thoughtfully organized, be pleasing to the senses, and include play spaces of interest. The setting should enforce an expectation of organization, which is modeled within children's tasks throughout the setting. For example, have children regularly organize bookshelves and play tools.

A child's environment should also be well prepared with the necessary tools to enable the day to unfold smoothly. For instance, as Billy walks through the door every morning, the pretty plants on the table make him smile. The attractive entryway gives him the boost he needs to start his routine. He proceeds to hang his coat and backpack on a hook set at his height, with his name and picture posted above it, which helps him feel connected to the classroom and in control of his belongings. As he settles in with his first activity, seeing his earlier work nicely displayed on the walls makes him feel competent and less anxious about the day.

Predictability also affects a child's actions and moods. A predictable environment has effective transitioning. Predictability in an environment occurs when children know what to expect and explanations to rules are simple and brief. For instance, "We walk in the halls." Furthermore, an environment that is predictable puts children at ease and gives them a sense of comfort and control. A predictable environment answers questions such as "What's going on now?" "What will happen next?" and "What purpose do different objects and areas serve?" Equipment and materials are consistently and predictably arranged throughout the environment, so children know what to do and how to get started in different areas. Boundaries such as shelves are kept low, transparent, and tidy to allow children to easily view their options and make choices. Entryways and exits are orderly, visually set apart, and inviting to children. A child's day remains consistent, while new activities are woven into established routines.

An organized environment also includes a child-friendly and consistent daily schedule that is balanced with active and quiet activities. This balance considers the natural ebb and flow of a child's energy, as a lack of regularly scheduled time for movement causes active bodies to explode into fidgetiness; without quiet time, frustration will peak. Post the daily schedule in a location where children can clearly see and understand it. If visuals are needed within the schedule for clarity, to increase a child's independence, or to manage an internalizing behavior such as anxiety, they should be creatively displayed.

The Environment Provides Choice

Choice within an environment is a powerful motivator for children—choice regarding *what they play* (puzzles or blocks), *how they play* (interactive video or sensory table), and *how they express what they learn through play* (drawing or reciting). Children play best when they have freedom to choose from a variety of challenging and creative activities, spaces, and tools with which to play and interact with their peers. Something as simple as allowing children the freedom to choose the color of paper they want to use on an art project increases their competence, security, and control. When giving children a voice through choice, they learn that they are valued and important, which plays a large role in how they sustain their play. Choice also increases a child's intrinsic motivation and builds a sense of purpose, identity, and desire to participate.

The environment should also offer continually rotating tool choices that are well organized and developmentally appropriate and do not rely on one single learning style, intelligence, or form of play. The next section discusses tools in more detail.

The Environment Effectively Integrates Play Tools

The best play tools for children stimulate their interests and imagination. They are open-ended and usable in many ways by children who possess various levels of development. Play tool choices should always be safe, durable, in working condition, and versatile and should inspire socialization. They should also be plentiful, as too few tools to choose from can stifle a child's play, yet too many choices can overwhelm or confuse a child. A balance is best; there should always be enough of a tool or duplicates to eliminate conflict over favored items. It is also important to regularly access an environment's play tools, gather new ones, and consider their play, learning, and sensory value.

For tools to work effectively in the environment, teachers must discuss their appropriate use with children, and the tools must be properly stored, well organized, and, when applicable, attractively displayed. An environment that effectively displays, discusses, and stores play tool choices orients children to options, promotes smooth cleanup and transitioning, and supports children who struggle with internalizing behaviors.

Children are more likely to share and sustain play when tools, especially those of high interest, are abundant, arranged pragmatically, and stored properly. Children should not have to venture across the room and back to get the play tools they have chosen for an activity. For example, place the water table next to the sink and hang

Suggestion for storing, discussing, and displaying materials	Benefit to Environment
Use both sides of shelving	◆ Low shelves that open both in front and in back are best for quick and easy access and to display objects at a child's eye level. • Consider children's mobility. For example, a child who uses a wheelchair may be unable to reach tools on shelves above or below arm's reach. ◆ Tools can be stored in plastic containers under shelving or tables. Although tools should have designated storage places, children should be allowed to use materials flexibly. • For example, if a child prefers to use blocks in an outdoor play area, the child should have the freedom to do so.
Store tools in appropriately sized containers	◆ Small, loose tools, such as manipulatives and crayons, are best stored in little bins, boxes, or shoeboxes. ◆ Baskets in a variety of colors and sizes are suitable for sorting and organizing supplies and add richness to the environment. Coffee cans are useful for storage. • For example, hold sharpened pencils in one can and after-use dull pencils in another. ◆ Containers should clearly display their contents when open and be the right size and shape for the space and items within. ◆ Storage should comfortably hold tools. Contents should not spill over. Lids should close properly and securely.

Limit and vary tool labeling	◆ Good storage is located near its point of use and is clearly and pleasingly labeled. ◆ Labels may consist of drawings, cut-out pictures, or computer clip art. ◆ Add tactile cues by gluing real objects to labels or using white glue to make raised drawings or words. ◆ For tools stored in cupboards or bins, put a photograph of the contents on the cupboard door or the front of the bin. ◆ Use moderation in labeling.
Store and display tools creatively	◆ To keep children interested, regularly rotate and attractively display tools. ◆ Use hooks mounted on a board and then tacked to the wall, or on a pegboard attached to the back of a shelf, to hang hats, bags, and dress-up clothes. ◆ Provide a shoe rack or hanging shoe bag to store shoes and small items. ◆ Display pots, pans, and safe kitchen utensils on a hanging rack. ◆ Use a small coat rack to hang bags, umbrellas, or bulky costumes. ◆ Hang three-tiered wire baskets or plastic storage bins from hooks for storing accessories such as costume jewelry. ◆ Store blocks according to shape and size. ◆ Store dress-up clothes in accessible, sturdy boxes or chests that children can open easily. ◆ Wash clothes regularly. ◆ Discard clothing that is tattered or missing too many fasteners.
Display and discuss guidelines	◆ Discuss with children, using pictures if needed, how tools should be properly used. ◆ Enforce responses when children choose to misuse materials. • For instance, "Treat book pages gently." Or "Water stays in the water table." ◆ Teach children to respectfully return materials to their proper place. ◆ Do not allow children to stuff tools away during cleanup or haphazardly leave them in any location.

Figure 8-5

Please consider . . .
Creatively Displaying Children's Work

Having a creative place in the environment to display children's work promotes self-expression, motivation, and a sense of community. Beautiful and well-organized displays of children's work also tell families and visitors what children are learning. Consider the following ideas for displays within the environment:

- Display children's work at children's eye level and regularly change displays. Outdated displays are ignored and become a distraction.
- Use pillars or the tops and backs of shelves to display work.
- Display work above countertops or on the fronts of children's desks.
- Hang work safely from ropes on the wall (use paper clips or pegs to attach work to the ropes).
- Display work on a blackboard, whiteboard, or wall space.
- Use easels, room dividers, a clothesline and clothespins, or fishnet.

smocks nearby. Regularly replace and refresh tools—throw away broken or worn-out tools and remove materials children have become bored with, such as puzzles that have become too easy. Whenever a play tool is added, replaced, or moved, point out the change to children.

Figure 8-5 offers suggestions to display, discuss, and store play tools effectively in the environment to promote creativity and choice.

The Environment Incorporates Richness

While children enjoy the security and comfort of predictability and continuity in their environment, they are also stimulated by novelty incorporated through richness. Richness in a setting involves the creation of liminal play spaces with elements of quirkiness expressed through their mood. Liminal spaces are mysterious or wondrous, provoking curiosity in children, without a single defined purpose. The mood of a play space is its emotional climate, or the energy it generates, which has a significant

Suggestions to Incorporate Richness

- Incorporate items that sparkle, glisten, glitter, and glow. Dollar stores are great resources for gathering inexpensive shiny and decorative things.
- Stock play spaces with an assortment of boxes, buckets, and bowls in a variety of shapes, colors, and sizes. Children can use these items as building supplies, as tools, or for other creations.
- Add furnishings and homelike touches, such as a welcome mat placed at the entryway or a Victorian-style, wall-mounted mirror positioned above the sink where children wash their hands.
- Provide heavy, thick, colorful towels for folding at a house play area.
- Various textured, colored, and patterned fabrics can stimulate a child's language development while adding richness. For example, use large pieces of burlap, cork, or silk to divide play areas.
- Place festive tablecloths on tables.
- Window displays, collages, or murals can be hung and bordered with contrasting colored fabric.

Figure 8-6

influence on a child's mental wellness and development. Size, function, layout, and décor all contribute to the mood of an environment and can be specifically set using an ambience of secrecy or myth to attract children. A space's mood should reflect how you want the child to feel when entering the space and playing in it. For example, quiet play spaces should release calm and peaceful feelings. The use of soothing instrumental music through headphones and softly textured quilts scented with lavender fragrances could help set such a mood.

Rich, liminal play spaces are neither one thing nor another; they are whatever a child needs or desires (Wilson 2010). The mood of a liminal play space is created with richness by connecting all of a child's senses. Merely placing a slow cooker or bread machine in a room to make soup or bake a loaf of bread not only produces a wonderful aroma but sets a positive mood. Something as simple as a mirror can intentionally create richness—for example, situating a three-way mirror or a raised walkway in a fantasy play area to make the space seem larger or positioning mirrors in front of or behind children so they can see their reflection while working. Flexibility and creativity are other aspects to consider when creating richness—for example, move a play area to another location in the environment to demonstrate flexibility. Figure 8-6 provides more ideas to incorporate richness into a child's environment.

Please consider . . .
How Sound Impacts the Environment

Sound can set the mood of a play space. For example, children can listen to their favorite music in the background while they play. Noise levels should remain moderate so that children can respond to one another and to environmental cues. Consider the following ideas regarding noise level within play spaces:

- Constant humming or buzzing from equipment is distracting; have the source of such sounds repaired or removed.
- Be aware of disruptive outside noise, such as construction sounds coming through open windows.
- Separate play spaces into noisy and quiet zones using drapes, carpets, partitions, and shelves. Too much noise can stifle play by distracting and overstimulating children.
- Choose décor carefully to soften sounds or confine noises. Mount corkboard or acoustic tile on walls or the ceiling to help absorb sound. Soft textures, such as carpet, rubber surfacing, and fabrics, absorb sound. Hard surfaces, such as tile flooring, reflect sound.
- High-pitched noises can be distressing and annoying, especially to children who have auditory sensitivities or struggle to concentrate.
- High noise levels can drain energy from children, desensitize their hearing, and impede communication and socialization.

The Environment Provides Various Integrated Play Spaces

Child care designer Anita Olds explains, "Varied [play] spaces prevent boredom, disinterest, and discomfort by enabling children to seek out activities and levels of stimulation to suit their moods and levels of arousal at different points in the day" (1989, 11). Children require a variety of integrated play spaces within their environment intended to support their overall development and mental wellness. For children who struggle with internalizing behaviors, several considerations must be identified for setting up and encouraging cathartic play, including distraction, seating, positioning, and tool adaption. Building on the preceding discussion of richness, play spaces should be organized so that specific activities can take place in specific areas, yet there is an interconnected ebb and flow between the spaces.

Play spaces should include various forms of creativity and self-expression using pathways of art, music, literacy, and movement. Sensory spaces with sand, water, and other natural items are essential as well. Use cultural, geographical, or historical themes to add variety and richness and to allow children to experience different places and eras. Because space is an important factor that affects children's play, eliminate overcrowding as much as possible, yet be sure to give special attention to each space's mood, seating, surfaces, and storage. Ultimately, be creative in space presentation and use, for example:

- Add variety to play spaces with diverse décor, such as differences in flooring.

Suggestions to Diversify Play Spaces

- Display colored vases filled with fresh flowers on a windowsill after wrapping them in cellophane to reflect sunlight.
- Vary tool softness, hardness, and size in play spaces. For example, place a large stuffed animal at a child-sized table set with a miniature tea set.
- Incorporate interesting visual puzzles, such as shapes and lines, arched doorways, hanging plants, fabric canopies, or spiraling mobiles.
- Integrate mystery and surprise via hidden nooks and crannies or mounds of sand or dirt where children can excavate buried "fossils."
- Use PVC pipe systems to make outdoor "telephones" for children to talk through.
- Provide a water table with funnels, bowls, oversized turkey basters, egg beaters, measuring cups and spoons, and paint and cooking brushes of all shapes and sizes.
- Include contrast within the environment, such as children working outdoors under a canopy amid a spring rain shower to create wet/dry contrast. Other contrasts to consider are up/down, moving/still, light/dark, hard/soft, and sunlit/shadowed.
- Provide cause-and-effect play opportunities, such as ice melting on black asphalt on a warm afternoon.
- Incorporate acoustic elements. For example, allow children to run a stick along a fence or railing to hear interesting sounds.

Figure 8-7

Please consider . . .
Using Music to Explore a Child's Moods

Use music to explore and enhance moods and emotions in children's play spaces:

- Play Frédéric Chopin's Polonaise in B Flat Major to stimulate a bold, dramatic mood.
- To set a more subdued mood, play "Ashokan Farewell" by Jay Ungar.
- Have children make musical instruments to use in active play areas. Easy-to-make instruments include
    - banjos
    - cardboard flutes
    - clappers
    - comb harmonicas
    - cymbals
    - homemade drums

For further suggestions, refer to page 155.

- Use carpet squares within the circle time area or a large area rug in the fantasy play area.
- Use bay window ledges, plastic crates, or old wooden boxes as seating.
- Create or expand a play space by attaching an easel to the back of a seldom-used storage closet door.
- Add diversity to play spaces by integrating richness, sensory stimulation, and exposure to nature.

See figure 8-7 for additional suggestions that can be used within indoor and outdoor environments.

The Environment Permits Privacy

Children have unique personalities and require regular time and space alone to nurture their abilities. Privacy gives children a sense of identity, satisfaction, and control. Having occasional access to a private space increases a child's intrinsic motivation and

Suggestions for Private Play Spaces

- A quiet and private retreat from distraction can be something simple:
  - a small spot under a towering willow tree
  - a warm windowsill seat
  - a small table with a sheet draped over it
- Spaces such as lofts, tents, and old bathtubs stuffed with pillows can provide not only privacy but a sense of comfort and control for children, especially when they need a quiet and secluded place to calm down.
- If a loft is constructed to provide a private space for children, consider how the space underneath will be used and supervised.
- Allow children to design and modify their own personal and private spaces, such as cubbies. Cubbies foster independence and teach children about their right to privacy, as well as that of others.
- Large cardboard boxes full of fuzzy cushions where a child can go to seek refuge after a long day make inexpensive private play spaces.

Figure 8-8

willingness to socialize. Children thrive when they are granted solitude in a secret spot to wander at their own pace or dawdle for a while. Robin Moore, author of *Childhood's Domain: Play and Place in Child Development*, defines "secret" as the special meaning children give to a place when they possess it deeply (2017, 478). This possession comes from hands-on interaction that lets children creatively make a spot their own. A secret and private place for children can be anywhere they feel independent and experience adventure and sensory stimulation, such as a desk, cubicle, carrel, or booth that children can create and keep in their control.

Within such private, safe, and controlled places, children can freely release their inner thoughts and feelings using various forms of play. On her blog, *Play Everything*, Morgan Leichter-Saxby asks how children are able to reflect on their private thoughts and feelings without private play time. "To be by oneself, in a place that feels safe and unadulterated, to have time and space to dive into the depths of the playing that is an intrinsic drive within you, to step at once aside from and yet deeper into the world as you experience it, that is when and where the richness of the play that is possible ripens to fruition," she writes (quoted in Wilson 2010, 28).

The Environment Offers Creativity and Self-Expression

The National Art Education Association and the National Association for the Education of Young Children emphasize the importance of the creative process in early

Please consider . . . Creating a Cardboard City

The Strong National Museum of Play inducted the cardboard box into its National Toy Hall of Fame in 2005. According to the museum's website, induction is based on the following criteria: *icon status* (the toy has wide recognition, respect, and remembrance), *longevity* (the toy remains popular and enjoyable generation after generation), *discovery* (the toy promotes learning, creativity, and discovery), and *innovation* (play is profoundly altered by the toy's design).

One idea for using cardboard boxes is to let children make a "cardboard city." With lots of time, cardboard boxes, tape, and support, children can create nearly anything. To watch a "cardboard city" in the making, watch the PBS documentary *Where Do the Children Play?*

For information about the documentary film and accompanying books, visit https://www.pgpedia.com/w/where-do-children-play.

Handout 14: Tools for Play Spaces, Creative Pathways, and Self-Expression

www.redleafpress.org/tpp/h-14.pdf

This handout provides simple and creative ideas for stakeholders to make children's play spaces more engaging with a variety of play tools.

Suggestions to Encourage Creativity and Self-Expression	Benefit to a Child's Development
Use odds and ends	◆ Where adults see junk, children see treasures and can be creative using low-cost objects. ◆ Ask families to donate items like these: • fabric • ribbon • leather • yarn scraps • corks and bottle caps • small containers • buttons and beads • costume jewelry ◆ Refer to page 192 for further possibilities.
Offer cardboard boxes	◆ Cardboard boxes stimulate creativity and promote spatial awareness, comfort, security, and control. ◆ Provide children access to boxes of various shapes and sizes to adapt to varied themes, such as castles, cars, or tunnels. ◆ Donated (unused) cardboard pizza boxes can help create a pizzeria play area.
Alternate and vary play tools	◆ For children to be creative, play tools should present increasing challenges throughout the year as they progress and grow in their development. ◆ Vary tools within categories. For example, blocks and other construction items should differ in weight, size, material, texture, and shape. ◆ Provide block variety such as foam, cardboard, and magnetic. ◆ Offer assorted puzzles. For example: • five-piece and fifteen-piece puzzles • wood inlay puzzles • three-dimensional puzzles • beginner jigsaw puzzles

Consider social value and cultural diversity	◆ Promote creativity and self-expression by offering diversity in • books • hats • puzzles • dolls • clothing that reflects various backgrounds ◆ Culturally diverse play tools promote self-esteem, acceptance, and unity. • Honor cultural differences by providing varied musical instruments from around the world, such as African hand drums and Hawaiian ukuleles. ◆ Display diverse replicas of artwork at a child's eye level around the environment so children can relate to their themes and learn about different parts of the world.
Offer modified and interchangeable play tools	◆ Provide play tools that are simpler, larger, less slippery, or color coordinated for children who may need extra support. • For example, provide a large wooden puzzle with secure knobs for children who struggle with flat pieces. ◆ Tools are also modified when they are integrated into different play spaces to extend a child's creativity. • For instance, one play space could encourage the process of seeing how many Lego bricks can be connected, while another asks children to create a Lego brick castle. ◆ Magnets at a gadget play area can be used at an art play space to design patterns on a magnetic board. • Pegboards find many uses during fantasy play—for example, they can transform into birthday candles and the board a birthday cake.
Provide play tools with tactile and auditory feedback	◆ Offer play tools that give children tactile and auditory feedback, such as letters made from heavy sandpaper. • Provide tools that meet children's specific sensory needs and add symbolism to their play. For example, storybooks can be accompanied by small objects relating to the story content, such as a small fuzzy teddy bear, a pair of doll overalls, and a large button for the book *Corduroy* by Don Freeman.
Use structured and unstructured play tools	◆ Make unstructured tools (such as sand or water) and structured tools (such as puppets) in a child's environment available to help them process uncomfortable emotions and anxiety-producing experiences. ◆ Animal play figures that often represent children's fears, such as snakes and spiders, should also be available. ◆ Consider whether the tools will be associated to any known ACEs in the children.

Figure 8-9

childhood curricula. Opportunities for cathartic play are possible when a child's environment encourages creativity and self-expression with tools such as dolls, blocks, and cardboard boxes. Children who have endured ACEs frequently seek out specific tools related to their emotional challenges and subconsciously attempt to transfer their inner distress through artwork or other offered creative means. In this way, creativity becomes an essential environmental element that helps children using what Freud called transference, as discussed on page 80.

Through creativity, children also gain confidence in their abilities, especially when they see their accomplishments attractively displayed throughout the room. Socially, when children are together in a creative environment that implements activities such as singing, dancing, and role playing, they learn to share and interact with one another. Figure 8-9 offers recommendations for encouraging creativity and self-expression. These ideas are intended to be part of a prescriptive tool kit to help children identify, channel, and manage their feelings as well as build healthy social skills.

◆◆◆◆◆

You should now be equipped to begin creating an environment that is appealing, stimulating, and emotionally safe for children who are experiencing internalizing behaviors. Consider the child's individual sensory needs and involve family. Family involvement tremendously increases the success rate of children undergoing EIIPS and is a significant factor in determining a child's healthy development.

Also significant is extending a child's play to the outdoors. The natural world arouses a child's senses, nurtures their reflective thinking, and naturally captures a child's interest and attention. The outdoors offers countless possibilities for play that can respond to a child's imagination and mobilize skills related to self-expression, creativity, problem solving, and emotional release. While this chapter discussed some ideas for incorporating the outdoors, chapter 9 is exclusively dedicated to nature, a restorative and essential environmental EIIPS element for children that enhances the internalizing behavior healing process.

9

Nature's Role in Supporting a Child's Mental Wellness

Play [in nature] is messy, unpredictable, spontaneous, freewheeling and sometimes a little scary. It looks a lot like life.

—Frances Heyck, secretary, Houston Adventure Play Association

Exposure to the natural world for exploration, discovery, and play, regardless of season, is essential. It affords children a feast for their senses—the sight of a clear blue sky, the smell of fresh rain, the sound of thunder, or the taste of falling snowflakes caught on the tongue. Nature is a feast of features, stimuli, and cathartic play opportunities for children experiencing internalizing behaviors. It should be considered an extension of a child's environment, and stakeholders are encouraged to provide daily, safe, challenging sensory interactions with nature and significant discovery time within it.

With a little planning and creativity, stakeholders can find various simple ways to expose children to nature, such as situating seating to face windows so children can feel incoming natural sunlight and fresh air on their faces or using containers to plant a small garden. Something as simple as watching the seasons change or smelling blooming spring flowers can benefit a child's mental wellness. Contact with such natural elements also positively influences a child's creative process and immune system.

This chapter is entirely devoted to the developmental and therapeutic benefits of play in nature for children and its role in EIIPS. It will outline how activities characteristically offered indoors can be extended to the natural world to enhance their sensory value and richness. Figure 9-1 offers some initial suggestions. Thereafter, the chapter will discuss the mental wellness benefits of extending a child's play to the natural world as well as child-preferred nature play spaces. It will conclude with ideas for cathartic play in nature.

Indoor Ideas to Expose a Child to Nature

- Display a well-lit aquarium with fish.
- Introduce a terrarium.
- Hang wind chimes or bird feeders.
- Plant brightly colored flowers in a window box to attract bugs.
- Provide a variety of tools like the following for children to use and interact with natural items:
  - magnifying glasses
  - binoculars
  - microscopes
  - telescopes
- Offer children chances like the following to experience the vagaries of nature:
  - being outdoors with umbrellas during a short burst of spring rain
  - watching rain wash away chalk on asphalt or dampen tree leaves
- Fill a nature corner with discovered treasures such as these:
  - wet clay
  - plant seedlings
  - toadstools
  - abandoned beehives
  - varied-sized chunks of bark and cut log slabs for rubbing, stripping, and imprinting

Figure 9-1

The Benefits of Playing in Nature

Nature has countless therapeutic rewards for children, and extending their play outdoors benefits both their mental wellness and their learning experiences. Nature nurtures resilience, promotes better sleep, and reduces symptoms of stress, anxiety, and depression.

Nature also promotes risk-taking: children love to challenge themselves to new and difficult adventures, and playing outside provides occasions to run faster, climb higher, and jump farther. Nature provides opportunities for open-ended play that can be risky and that gives children chances to develop and master new skills. It gives children opportunities to explore, question, and develop theories about how things work (Kinsner 2019). It allows them to experience challenging weather conditions, such as blustery winds, thick fog, and wet morning dew.

Other benefits of nature on a child's development and well-being are well supported:

- Contact with nature improves a child's self-discipline, particularly in areas of concentration, impulse control, and delayed gratification.
- Playing regularly in nature makes children less susceptible to illness and better able to regulate their emotions.
- Nature enables children's play to be more imaginative, diversified (enabling richer language), independent, and social.
- Playing in nature reduces (or eliminates) antisocial behavior, including aggression and bullying.
- Nature draws children together, encourages friendships, and bolsters childhood resilience (Roberts et al. 2019; Ernst et al. 2019).

It is therefore beneficial to create outdoor play spaces for children, keeping at the forefront their preferences, environmental needs, and safety. Each area's mood and purpose should be specific and well prepared.

Child-Preferred Play Spaces in Nature

Children have a general proclivity for naturalized play spaces (Donison 2018). They are drawn to nature's limitless sensorial play opportunities, such as thick hedges to hide in, bushes against fences to build forts around, and lush grass to run in. Children's play spaces should capitalize on their interests and be full of favored nature items, such as plants, trees, flowers, water, dirt, sand, mud, bugs, and pond creatures like frogs and tadpoles. Ensure that children learn to treat tiny creatures with respect and

Please consider . . .
Open-Ended Materials and Features

Outdoor play spaces should offer a variety of features with limitless possibilities and open-ended materials to challenge children in testing themselves, cooperating, and finding creative solutions to problems. For instance, a child's access to water can be as simple as a hose or small water table. Additional suggestions include the following:

- hills
- plants, especially mammoth sunflowers
- stages
- pathways
- sand and digging areas
- hideouts
- sound (refer to the *Please Consider* . . . box on page 134)
- open areas to run
- seating
- gardens that demonstrate diversity, such as stalks of corn, pumpkin patches, and themed herb areas (spearmint, peppermint, chocolate mint)
- artwork, such as sculpture, murals, and/or mosaics

gentle handling. Because children tend to gravitate toward messy mudholes rather than sophisticated play contraptions, their play places should also be full of activity and motion supporting fantasy, constructive, and manipulative play as well as social interaction, ambiguity, richness, and variety in structure and design.

Children benefit from varied play zones of different sizes and formalities, such as spaces that are intimate, secure, enclosed, and hidden. In short, they require spaces! Open spaces; quiet, small spaces; spaces for group play; and spaces for solo play, to name a few. Such variety encourages children to engage in different forms of play and interactions. The upcoming section outlines recommendations for child-preferred play spaces in nature that offer this sort of diversity.

Please consider . . .
Using Sound to Complement Outdoor Play

Rusty Keeler, author of *Natural Playscapes: Creating Outdoor Play Environments for the Soul,* offers three ideas for incorporating sound in a way that complements outdoor play areas:

- Use sound as a *backdrop* to play—for example, hang wind chimes of various sizes and materials, such as wood and metal.
- Use sound as a *by-product* of play—for example, add cowbells and rattles that make noise when children enter or leave a play space.
- Use sound as the *goal* of play—for example, include a metal drum, giant marimba, or gong in an outdoor area for children to bang on (Keeler 2008).

Play Spaces in Nature That Encourage Physical Activity

Children learn and retain more when they're moving and their senses are fully engaged. Spaces in nature that promote active and creative movement are ideal for children experiencing internalizing behaviors, allowing them to release pent-up emotions—especially anger and frustration. An active nature play area is typically large and open with well-defined boundaries, as outlined on page 114. In active outdoor play spaces, children have a variety of balls for outdoor games, tricycles for riding on pathways, and various sizes of wagons and pails for transporting dirt. The space has ample room for running and equipment such as beams available for climbing or tires for swinging. Foot pathways made of stepping-stones for children to balance on connect different play areas, often passing by beautifully colored plants and flowers woven throughout the environment.

Ideas for Play Spaces in Nature That Encourage Physical Activity

- Offer large pieces of driftwood or untreated lumber for children to balance and climb on.
- Create hopscotch games using colored chalk on concrete pathways.
- Ask a local farm or feed store to donate hay bales for fort building, climbing, or balancing. (Note: Consider children's allergies before using hay.)
- Solicit volunteers to bring in smooth river boulders for children to climb on.
- Ask for donations of approved industrial-sized piping for children to crawl through.
- Incorporate available slopes and hills of varying steepness for children to roam, roll down, and socialize on, or try cardboard sledding.
- Allow children to use megaphones in wide-open outdoor spaces.
- Use tires for outdoor play. Tires are economical and versatile pieces of outdoor equipment usable for swinging, climbing, or making a sand pit.
  - When tires are used for swings, holes should be drilled in the bottom to prevent water from collecting and allowing mosquitoes to breed and fester.
- Climbing structures and paths with a variety of entries, exits, and levels provide amazing gross-motor, movement, and active play adventures for multiple children.
- Create an outdoor "romper room" for children by offering mats of different densities, including safety mats at least four inches thick.
  - Encourage children to roll, tumble, and fall on the mats.
  - Provide giant exercise balls, hippity-hop balls (bouncer balls with handles), and large balls for bouncing and catching.
  - Set up a bowling game with soft, oversize pins and balls.
  - Be sure to regularly sanitize mats.
- Provide scooter boards, Hula-Hoops, and a CD player with varied musical selections to encourage marching and dancing.
- Create a space for children to jump, throw, and play catch using balls of various shapes, sizes, textures, and weights.
  - Offer beanbags and soft foam basketballs with containers such as laundry baskets for targets.
  - Have children throw and catch balls independently, adding to the game by having children throw a ball in the air, clap, and then catch it.
  - Encourage socializing by having children catch and throw beanbags and balls with a partner.
- Create outdoor tunnels for children, using recycled barrels and large cardboard boxes to encourage a variety of cooperative games such as hide-and-seek.
  - Recycled plastic barrels make excellent climbing equipment. Fasten a fat barrel to a wooden base to form a tunnel to climb through.
  - Decorate the boxes and barrels with different materials for tactile purposes.

Figure 9-2

Concerning footpaths, to make them more physically challenging, place the stones beyond children's normal stepping distance so they must jump from one to the next. To increase socialization opportunities for children experiencing internalizing behaviors, arrange the stones in an irregular pattern, as if they were situated in a river, and challenge children to cross the river without falling in. Encourage them to help each other make it across by holding hands to jump from stone to stone. Use beams, low benches, mounted ladders, climbing nets, ropes, hanging bars, or a set of rings for outdoor climbing and balancing as well. Plant mint or other pleasant-smelling herbs around the logs. Scatter bark chunks, soft wood chips, mulch, or straw around the logs; erect railings for children who need balancing help. Other ideas for play spaces in nature that encourage physical activity are listed in figure 9-2.

Play Spaces in Nature That Nurture Quiet Retreat

A richly designed play space in nature where children can retreat for a quiet, contemplative moment to read, create art, or engage in scientific observations supports their emotional well-being. A little hideaway under a tree can provide a sanctuary for a child to calm down and recharge in the beauty of the outdoors. Play spaces in nature that foster solitude offer children more focused activities, such as reading, painting at an easel, doing a puzzle, playing board games, or working with manipulatives. These spaces should be secluded, be out of the way of heavy traffic flow, and offer a cozy, homelike feel. For example, a hill—nothing more than a patch of elevated grass, off to the side—can become a quiet area for a child to sit and reflect. A net swing or hammock can also act as a solitary spot for children to refocus and unwind.

For many children, relaxation is achieved actively rather than passively. Hence, climbing into a quiet tree house refuge may be an excellent way to let off steam and relax. Many children love to chase butterflies, so consider incorporating a butterfly garden into a quiet outdoor play space. (Be sure to have butterfly nets available.) Bonsai gardens are another idea for a quiet outside play area that promotes entrance into new cultures. Other ideas for play spaces in nature that nurture quiet retreat include those listed in figure 9-3, or visit www.thegardenhelper.com for outdoor garden and play area ideas.

Ideas for Play Spaces in Nature That Nurture Quiet Retreat

- Designate a quiet spot as a refuge for listening to music and nature sounds.
- Provide a recording of sounds such as rain and thunder, wind, birds, or crickets for children to listen to.
- Hang a canopy of netting over and around the refuge. String leaves, bells, and flowers throughout the area.
- Allow children a quiet place to listen to audiobooks. Provide a battery-operated music player and headphones.
- Offer a microphone for children to read aloud and hear their voices as they follow along.
- Place stumps or crates in the area for children to sit on.
- Fill a box or crate with a variety of instruments like these for children to experiment with:
  - an autoharp
  - a gourd rattle
  - a small keyboard
  - a child-sized guitar
  - homemade coconut cymbals
  - a variety of kazoos
  - flutes
  - an assortment of handbells, old kitchen pots and pans, and small bongo drums
- Lofts make great quiet nature play areas for private socializing or doodling in a special journal.
  - Provide ramps for access instead of ladders or steps, if possible.
  - Lofts require close supervision; consider how the space underneath will be used.
  - Lofts can also become areas for visual stimulation—such as with flashlights, shadows, and soft lighting—and for distinguishing other differences, such as temperature, sounds, materials, and textures.

Figure 9-3

Play Spaces in Nature That Inspire Creativity

Inspire creativity by designing your outdoor play space using mud, paint, and other sensory-oriented materials. Studies show that water and sand are two natural play elements that children prefer that also improve their creativity (Acar 2014). Therefore, play areas in nature should promote their use in various forms, such as sand pits and water tables. Spaces that inspire creativity are commonly messy and stocked with creative tools, both natural and otherwise. Children can dig for worms, look under rocks for roly-polies (pill bugs), or plant herb gardens. It is best for these play areas to be situated near a hose or outdoor sink, though rainy days may make this unnecessary.

Rainy-day play also reaches out to children's creativity, transforms play spaces, and allows sensory play to emerge in endless ways. For example, children will love making

Ideas for Play Spaces in Nature That Inspire Creativity

- Water troughs or large, clean plastic 55-gallon barrels provide a contained area for messy play.
  - Turn barrels into tunnels or cut them in half and create ponds or troughs for water play.
- Sprinkle powdered paint or food coloring into rain puddles on pathways, then use brooms to sweep the water and mix colors.
- When possible, let children walk barefoot in lush grass or sun-warmed rain puddles.
- Fashion benches out of the solid earth or fallen logs for children to have a contemplative sitting spot to quietly observe nature.
- Add sound through wind chimes, bells, or pinwheels that can whistle in the wind.
- Add a kitchen to a sand pit to invite sensory play by putting in a realistic toy oven or old sink.
- Use pallets, plastic milk crates, and other recycled items in play areas.
- Offer big buckets and pails so children can transport natural items.
- Dirt, sand, and mud inspire creative play.
- Add a cluster of boulders and rocks with a stream of water cascading between or below the rocks to prompt a richer play setting.
- Obstacle courses challenge children and spark creativity.
  - Create a course in which children must engage in various challenges: climbing under and over, sliding down, jumping across, tumbling through, pushing, pulling, balancing.
- Provide old tarps, sheets, and tents for children to use in building shelters, dens, or play tunnels.
- Offer a variety of blocks, bricks, and rocks for children to create waterways, bridges, and pathways across mud puddles.

Figure 9-4

Please consider . . .
The Interactive Power of Plants

Because of their interactive properties, plants stimulate discovery, dramatic pretend play, and imagination. They speak to all of a child's senses, so it's not surprising that children are closely attuned to environments with vegetation. Plants in a pleasant environment with a mix of sun, shade, color, texture, fragrance, and softness also encourage a sense of peacefulness. Plants beautify and add richness to a child's environment. Plants are vital.

You can even use ecological theming with vegetation to create the identity of a play area. For example, an interactive water play station can be set in a bog or stream habitat. It is also important to incorporate ecological areas that use indigenous vegetation and settings so children can experience, learn about, and develop an appreciation of their local environment. When selecting plants, take the following into consideration:

- Choose plants of different shapes and sizes with different leaves and flowers.
- Provide interesting variations in color and characteristics for children to explore, such as sunflowers, snapdragons, and natural herbs.
    - Sunflowers come in various colors and sizes and offer seeds for children to roast.
    - Snapdragons also come in different colors and sizes, and children enjoy pinching their blossoms to make the "dragon mouth" part of the flower open.
    - Natural herbs such as mint are easy for children to plant and harvest and come in numerous varieties, such as peppermint, lemon, and chocolate.
    - Natural herbs can also be set up indoors as an indoor herb garden planted in jars or pots.
    - Dill is another herb most children like; not only does it smell like pickles, but it has feathery-looking foliage that interests them.

For additional ideas for child-friendly and nonpoisonous plants for play and learning, consult Robin C. Moore's *Plants for Play: A Plant Selection Guide for Children's Outdoor Environments.*

mud soup or painting with mud on white sheets hung on a clothesline. Invest in spare umbrellas, rain boots, and raincoats for children to use for rainy-day outdoor play. See figure 9-4 for more ideas.

Ideas for Cathartic Play in Nature

Nature play contains a hidden cathartic curriculum that draws children outdoors and richly lends itself to meeting their mental wellness needs. Incorporating nature into children's daily activities to promote EIIPS is ideal. In doing so, keep in mind that almost any indoor activity can be modified for the outdoor environment. Thus, when considering and creating nature play spaces and opportunities for children, focus on nature's healing elements—for example, how natural sunlight can positively influence a child's creative process.

Furthermore, provide various play spaces that offer a range of activities for children to practice skills to develop their competence and confidence, both of which have implications for development. For example, encourage risk-taking with the use of landscaping and varying ground levels that present spots for children to climb on or crawl under. Including risk-taking activities as part of nature play is important because it builds resilience, especially for children from challenging backgrounds. Play spaces in nature that encourage risk-taking permit children to encounter challenges in a safe setting where they begin to learn about boundaries. This is also key in extending a child's physical prowess and, by extension, independence. For example, a carefully situated obstacle course using natural resources can stimulate children to be courageous and challenge sensory pattern differences.

Additional points to remember:

- Provide shelter and shade, nooks and crannies, and overviews of the play yard and its structures.
- Use nature's color and diversity when creating nature play opportunities. Consider visual, physical, and sensory cues embedded along passageways, within gardens, on top of surfaces, and written on colorful signs.
- Integrate flowers and other plants, as suggested on page 139, using textures, shades, and smells to stimulate or challenge children's senses.
- Offer plenty of creative play tools. As in indoor play, tools for outdoor play should rotate with the seasons and region.
- As much as possible, insert natural resources such as dirt piles, fallen logs, boulders, water, and sand into play scenarios to encourage socializing and pathways to creativity and self-expression.

Building on these points, the previous information in this chapter, and the cathartic powers of play as outlined in chapter 6, the upcoming pages suggest ideas to address and prevent internalizing behaviors. The ideas are indicative of children's individualized developmental needs and intended to match play's curative factors to the child's needs; you will need to customize the nature play you provide for children struggling with internalizing behaviors. Together with balanced play space plans, diverse arrangements, and the benefits of nature's healing properties, stakeholders can design and offer children play spaces in nature that are personally themed according to interests; cater to unique formulas and sensory needs; and give children opportunities to practice social and self-regulation skills as well as process and channel uncomfortable feelings.

Magnification play: Children are fascinated by small-scale wildlife, such as ladybugs, caterpillars, grasshoppers, and beetles. Outdoor magnification play allows children the chance to watch such smallness right before their eyes. Have children collect pebbles, stones, gravel, shells, and other natural objects for magnification play. Children can examine natural items like locust and snail shells, seeds, acorns, pine cones, flowers, and leaves with various magnifying glasses, color paddles, and prisms. Children can arrange and sort these items by various characteristics, including size, texture, color, shape, and markings. Stakeholders can also help children focus on the details of smallness during magnification play by narrowing their field of vision with a cardboard-tube "telescope" or using a Hula-Hoop to section off areas of lush grass. With guided focusing, a bed of moss can become a miniature forest, or ants carrying their cargo can be closely observed.

Trench play: Trench play is perfect for messy outdoor play, and plastic rain trenching is available inexpensively at any building supply store, lumberyard, or hardware store. This is ideal for children because it is lightweight and smooth, and its curved surfaces make it safe to work with. Attach trenching vertically, horizontally, and in zigzags to a wall (with permission). Children can pour sand and water down and enjoy rolling balls, marbles, or pea gravel through the trenches. Add pitchers, pots, buckets, and stepladders for more options. Trench play teaches physics concepts and ignites social interaction—children can work together to search for what they can pour in and catch coming out of the trenches.

Boat play: Place an old rowboat or canoe in the play yard or partially bury it in the ground. Add creative boat-related accessories, such as play fishing poles, nets, and tackle boxes full of rubber worms, tied flies, and fishing lures (with hooks removed). To promote pirate adventures, mount a wheel from an old stroller (preferably a large, fat, all-terrain wheel) as a steering wheel for the boat. Add a telescope and walking plank. Make a wooden raft out of donated two-by-fours—offer realistic illustrations of rafts and canoes through books, paintings, or posters for children who have never seen either.

Clothesline play: Erecting an old-fashioned clothesline is a simple and low-cost way to incorporate outdoor fantasy play for children. Concepts such as wet and dry, heavy and light, and sinking and floating can be reinforced during such play. Recruit a volunteer to construct a clothesline using concrete, poles sunk into the ground, and line. Position poles and lines low enough for children to get blankets over but high enough so that no one runs into the line. Once it's up, provide a laundry basket full of donated clothes from different cultures for children to wash and pin up with different-sized and -colored clothespins. For variety, on hot spring days, dampen the clothing or let children wash heavily textured clothes, such as denim, in huge pails and old washtubs. Other possibilities include:

- Securely mount old-fashioned washboards for children to wash clothing.
- Let children paint by clipping large sheets of paper to the clothesline. Mix thin paint in spray bottles or provide a variety of paintbrushes.

Wood bench play: Set up a wood bench area stocked with scrap lumber, pallets, and other rot-resistant pieces of wood as a space for children to safely explore and investigate the form and function of real hand tools. Here children can practice twisting, turning, sawing, and filing, all of which support their fine-motor and eye-hand coordination skills and development. Free scrap lumber is usually available at local home improvement stores and lumberyards.

Consider age-appropriateness when providing sandpaper, child-sized carpentry tools, and safety goggles. Offer soft Styrofoam blocks to pound things into before moving on to hard wood. Include a low workbench with a trough or a tree stump of soft wood for hammering. Install a tool display on the wall and bins for different-sized scraps of wood. Consider placing a wood bench in a separate, low-traffic area to minimize the loss of small supplies. Store tools and supplies, such as various grains of wood, bark, sawdust, plywood, shingles, wood shavings, and tree rings, safely and securely. Hang birdhouses or other woodwork. Before inserting a wood bench play option into the environment, host an interactive safety lesson with students. Go over tools and proper use of the area.

Gadget play: Outdoor gadget play offers children the opportunity to unravel the mystery of how things work. They will enjoy the clink and clank of an old typewriter as they try to figure out its parts or learn by tinkering and toying with a nonfunctional toaster. By working with real, safely disabled and discarded items, children learn sequencing, patterns, organization, measurement, and spatial awareness. Offer an assortment of plumbing equipment to explore, like faucets and lengths of plastic and metal piping. Provide a variety of belts, hats, and aprons for children to wear. Let them explore different ways to use measuring cups and other mathematical instruments. Figure 9-5 provides additional suggestions to ignite gadget play.

Discovery play: A nature discovery play space provides an area where children can explore themes that interest them and increase their background knowledge. Outdoors, this area can be situated under a canopy or within a gazebo and include books on many subjects. If possible, add an old set of encyclopedias, Childcraft books, and/or magazines such as *Ranger Rick*, *Zoobooks*, and *Your Big Backyard*. Pottery and other clay objects, tuning forks, and magnetic wands can also be displayed on a table within the play space. Add architectural pictures and an assortment of tactile and

Gadget Play Ideas

- broken clocks and walkie-talkies
- washers and screws
- handheld vacuums
- plastic safety goggles
- old rotary and cell phones
- locks with linking keys
- small ramps with tiny cars
- an assortment of kaleidoscopes
- unusable cameras
- levers and pulleys
- nuts and bolts
- old microwaves
- measuring tapes and rulers
- scales (balance, platform, digital)
- radios of various sizes, makes, and models
- magnets in all shapes, colors, and sizes

Figure 9-5

Please consider . . .
Other Ideas for Cathartic Play in Nature

Here are some additional creative suggestions to prescriptively individualize cathartic play in nature for a child with an internalizing behavior:

- **Make mazes.** Make a maze or tunnel from several different-sized boxes. Cut windows in the box sides and put play tools of personal interest to the child inside. Add an assortment of flashlights and beautifully illustrated books.
- **Build blockbusters.** Fill a box with alluring blocks and a variety of different-sized play tools, such as dinosaurs and jungle animals. Add several fabric blocks and prism blocks. Prism blocks are transparent building blocks that radiate color when light passes through them. Fabric blocks are soft and can have pictures on them. Fabric blocks can be magnetized by splitting their seams and inserting super-duty magnets and then restitching. The blocks will then be usable for stacking and attaching. For additional "blockbuster" ideas, visit Fat Brain Toys at www.fatbraintoys.com.
- **Fiddle with "tinker" toys.** Children enjoy taking things apart or tinkering with them. As suggested on page 142, make a variety of safely disabled appliances available in a corner or a side table. Children can also tinker with ramp experiments or bridge work with small cars. A simple manual juicer is another useful tinker item: have the child put the juicer together, juice a few oranges, take it apart, and clean it in soapy water. Using a Tinkertoys construction toy set, a favorite for generations, is another idea.

visual props, such as postcards from around the world. Include various literacy tools, including pencils, markers, and crayons, as well as large and small colored note cards and journals for children to write, draw, and record their research findings in other ways. For further discovery ideas, read *The Magic of the Stump Pile* by Julie Bookwalter and Veronika Vicqueneau.

◆◆◆◆◆

These methods will help stakeholders expose children to the healing elements of the natural world and create play spaces within it that ignite creativity and self-expression. The natural world is a cathartic resource for internalizing behaviors using all forms of play, and we can use its naturally occurring interactive props and stages to our advantage. Nature has the potential to tremendously support, prevent, and intervene upon internalizing behaviors when we use its natural resources and textures like sand, dirt, and water. In combination with other creative materials, such as cardboard boxes, a child's creativity, self-expression, senses, emotions, and social skills are stimulated.

Because early childhood is a critically formative period, contact with nature's numerous cathartic elements is encouraged. Ultimately, children experiencing internalizing behaviors require an environment that respects their individuality, addresses emotional struggles, challenges them, allows choices, and engages them in favored activities to socialize with their peers. Children also need the freedom to explore their feelings and learn to manage them. The natural world affords endless opportunities to meet such requirements.

10

Pathways to Creativity and Self-Expression

The two main continuities in child's play are the quest for autonomy and the demonstration of creativity.

—Howard Chudacoff

The way children express themselves is typically reflective of their development, their environment, and how prepared the environment is to cater to their unique formulas. Pathways to creativity and self-expression, referred to as *pathways* from this point forward for the sake of convenience, are cathartic play ideas infused with the creative process and the cathartic elements of nature to implement EIIPS for children struggling with internalizing behaviors. Pathways such as drawing and painting act as vehicles to release and process painful emotions and experiences; they are also recognized as effective approaches to healing and supporting children who struggle with depression, anxiety, and social challenges.

This section is intended to enhance the suggestions in the previous chapters and encourage their potential to empower children to use their imagination and unique formulas in personally fulfilling ways. When stakeholders incorporate pathways as part of EIIPS, they give children the opportunity to tap into the cathartic powers of play, become active participants in their healing process, and learn the needed skills to process, manage, and master the uncomfortable feelings and thoughts that frequently accompany internalizing behaviors. At times, medication accompanies this route, and the activities suggested are not advocated as a replacement for medication. Using medication for depression and anxiety with young children remains in need of significant research; stakeholders are encouraged to proceed with extreme caution in this area. For further study on the topic, refer to the following resources:

- *Psychiatric Disorders: Current Topics and Interventions for Educators* by Paul C. McCabe and Steven R. Shaw
- National Institute of Mental Health (NIMH), 2008 Mental health medications (NIH Publication No. 02-3929)

What Are Pathways to Creativity and Self-Expression?

The pathways described in this chapter are a means for children experiencing an internalizing behavior to develop healthy social and emotional regulation skills, become aware of their feelings, build an emotional vocabulary to express and manage them, and find useful ways to confront co-occurring conditions that stem from painful experiences, emotions, and physical reactions. Stakeholders are encouraged to lock into children's unique formulas and interests when selecting from the many pathway forms and delivery methods available, as presented in figure 10-1.

Pathways to creativity and self-expression have cathartic value for children experiencing internalizing behaviors for several reasons. For one, they are a natural language for most children and can be a valuable modality in enhancing expression of trauma, distress, or loss. Further discussion supporting pathways as EIIPS is presented in the next section, followed by pathway suggestions. For purposes of clarity within the chapter, pathways are framed within

- secure attachments (see chapter 3);
- an emotionally safe and comfortable environment with essential elements as presented in chapter 8, particularly family involvement;

- creative, sensory-driven, nature-oriented play tools that are personalized for the child's unique formula and recognize the child's individual differences in terms of abilities; and
- a comprehensive focus on the *whole* child.

Forms and Delivery Methods of Pathways to Creativity and Self-Expression	
Visual arts	drawing, painting, sculpting, or other means for a child to visually represent inner thoughts and emotions
Literature	journaling, doodling, poetry, storytelling, interactive reading
Music	playing a musical instrument, listening to music, composing a song
Cooking	baking, frosting, garnishing, or other food preparation processes
Drama/dance	role playing, dramatic play with costumes, interpretive dance, yoga
Exploration	inventing, tinkering with gadgets, gardening, building

Figure 10-1

Pathways for EIIPS

The American Academy of Neurology considers pathways as a best wellness practice. The American Dance Therapy Association and American Music Association both recommend pathways for children who struggle with internalizing behaviors. Additionally, large amounts of literature support the theory that therapies emphasizing movement, play, and creativity are enormously effective in treating and supporting the social and emotional needs of children (Smith et al. 2020; Degges-White 2020). Pathways are ideal for EIIPS because they permit children to channel their thoughts and feelings to express emotional turmoil in a manner other than speaking words alone.

Pathways stimulate neurological processes that, when combined with child-tailored creative methods, can be useful in overcoming intrusive thoughts and feelings often at the root of internalizing behaviors. Additionally, each pathway has unique

EIIPS properties, roles, and integral differences, meaning you can tailor your choices to the application, the objective, and the child's unique formula. For example, drawing is conducive to the privacy and independence needed for a child who is deeply depressed, while music via pathways of singing and playing instruments encourages the socialization that may be essential for a child who is withdrawn and anxious.

Pathways should be an integrated part of an early childhood curriculum, and children's created works should be respected and treated as reflections of their unique formulas, especially when evaluated. The following pages present pathway launching points for stakeholders to use with children experiencing internalizing behaviors, along with brief descriptions to implement, modify, complement, and catapult additional strategies within the individual internalizing behavior sections. Regardless of form, pathways are meant to activate a child's senses, facilitate self-discovery, and propel change. Keep in mind that while a child's final "masterpiece" individually reflects that child, what is more important is the cathartic benefit of the process the child took to complete it.

Please consider . . .
The Three Pathway Processes

It's important for children to have ample time and opportunities to nurture their creativity and self-expression using various pathway processes. Pathway processes not only fuel a child's creativity and self-expression but accelerate their development. Providing expressive, unstructured activities frees children to follow the dictates of their intuition. The possible pathways are numerous and can easily be geared toward children's interests.

Creative processes are grouped within three categories:

1. **Application:** drawing, sketching, stenciling, coloring, gluing, cutting, stamping, and painting
2. **Formation:** clay/dough modeling, collage, wire art, sand tray, papier-mâché, origami, carpentry, jewelry, and mask making
3. **Stitchery:** sewing, lacing, tapestry art, and nature weaving, like branch weaving

Drawing and Painting

Drawing and painting provide "self-soothing" experiences for children. A simple sheet of white paper can become a safe place for children to express themselves in a nonthreatening manner, whether by a simple line or paintbrush stroke or imaginative curves and shapes. Consequently, it is worthwhile to implement a drawing journal in which children can "squiggle" with a daily new line, such as zigzag, wavy, dotted,

Drawing and Painting Pathway Ideas

- Draw a picture together with a child. Draw the first line, and have the child draw the second line. Continue until the masterpiece is complete.
  - For creativity, use gel pens, feather pens, weighted pens, and vibrating pens. Do the same with paint, one stroke of paint per person at a time.
  - Extend the collaborative drawing or painting outdoors onto windows, easels, or a sheet-draped clothesline.
- Crayons, markers, and colored pencils can be used in place of pencils and pens. Provide a variety of colors, including those that represent various skin tones.
- Let children try finger or large triangle crayons.
- Make glitter, metallic, and wacky colors available. Crayola has zany and scented products children will enjoy, such as Dragon Drool Red and Belching Baboon Yellow.
- Use ultra-thin and thick felt markers, colored chalks, and marker paint bottles.
- For surface variety, use the floor or let children kneel or sit on a small stool. Use different paper surfaces as well: construction paper, copy/computer paper, butcher paper, cardboard, foil.
- Offer an Etch-a-Sketch for drawing. (You might consider Etch-a-Sketch minis, which are less bulky.)
- Take children outside and have them look for a variety of shapes to sketch.
- Ask children enhancing and discriminating questions to stimulate their thoughts as they draw their pictures.
- Let children make drawings with yarn or allow them to draw or paint on waxed paper, on a cookie sheet, or in sensory bins filled with shaving cream or fingerpaint.
- Children can also "draw" pictures on each other's backs or arms with their eyes closed.
- Lego promotes creative emotion drawing activities for children. And Next Comes L and other websites have a wealth of ideas.

Figure 10-2

jagged, stair-stepped, or straight. While they are drawing in their journals, give children the chance to share their work. For children who are reluctant to share or struggling to interact, try using a simple conversation starter with them. For example: "Each of us will have a piece of paper and a pencil. I will draw a squiggle, and you will make any kind of drawing out of it you would like to share with me or your friends."

For ideas on how to do squiggle drawings, see figure 10-2 or visit websites such as Sugar, Spice & Glitter.

Storytelling

Storytelling enables several methods for children to safely express their emotions. When children who are experiencing internalizing behaviors become storytellers, they do reparative work, namely, on their self-confidence. Performed properly, this facilitates the expression of difficult emotions in a nonconfrontational manner (Rose 2020). A pertinent point to consider when using storytelling is how to link the selected story and the child's emotional experiences. Think about the emotions you want to communicate, and then craft the story to support that emotion, using appealing visuals or props.

Storytelling, as it pertains to this section as well as throughout the text, refers to using storybooks as tools to facilitate pathways. Freud (1912) dealt successfully with the subject of literature, stories, and reading in the psychological development of children. During storytelling, stakeholders and children read materials aloud together, followed by engaging in another pathway, such as drawing or painting, in a way that is related to the story.

Please consider . . .
Social and Movement Stories

Social stories are short stories describing a situation, concept, or social skill relevant to the child's need. They are effective because they provide more personalized support for children. For social story examples and further resources, consult One Place for Special Needs (http://www.oneplaceforspecialneeds.com).

Movement stories encourage children to explore storytelling through music and movement concepts, such as pantomiming and theater games, which help children develop physical, social, and emotional skills. They are useful starting points for improvisation and exploration of story content through sound, rhythm, and drama. For ideas, refer to *Movement Stories for Young Children: Ages 3–6* by Helen Landalf and Pamela Gerke.

Storytelling is beneficial for helping children develop social and emotional regulation as well as attention and comprehension skills. It also provides children opportunities for solving emotional challenges such as jealousy, anger, or fear. Through different genres and literacy resources, such as interactive big books, poetry, chants, songs, story boards with felt, and story mitts, storytelling can be used in numerous ways for EIIPS. You might have children draw pictures of favorite scenes or characters from stories or think up different endings to stories. Children can participate in interactive and imaginative games linked to stories or perform skits, role-play characters, and predict how a story might continue after the ending. Storytelling can be a one-on-one activity or a group activity with multiple copies of the same book. Series and books to consider for storytelling include *Amazing Grace* by Mary Hoffman, the Franklin the Turtle books by Paulette Bourgeois, the Berenstain Bears books by Jan and Stan Berenstain, and the Llama Llama books by Anna Dewdney.

Encourage various pathways for storytelling at home as well. For example, send a creative newsletter home, sharing the activities. Figure 10-3 lists additional ideas.

Music and Movement

For purposes of clarity, within this section *music* and *movement* act as one entity, not two separate ones. Moving creatively and self-expressively to music, playing instruments while dancing, experimenting with play tools that make sounds, singing, and giving musical demonstrations are all pathways for children that foster development and give voice to their inner world. Together music and movement stimulate children's senses and act as a powerful medium for them to safely explore their feelings. They also serve as an exciting way to introduce children to other cultures, languages, and traditions and musical styles. A listing of musical suggestions can be found on page 155.

Music and movement boost self-confidence, improve concentration, and reduce anxiety. They create a haven for children to enhance their social development through literacy and language. For instance, when children participate in music-integrated lessons such as those mentioned above, their literacy skills improve, enabling them to build a strong emotional language through which they can find the right words to identify their thoughts and feelings.

Music and movement also promote active listening, an important social skill, especially when participating in group games such as musical chairs. Musical group games help children develop and practice self-control over their bodies. To practice both active listening and controlled behavior, play Stomp: using the guidelines of the game Red Light, Green Light, have children stomp on large, securely placed circles made from bubble wrap as music is played. "Green light" means stomp on the circles; "red light" means no stomping. Figure 10-4 provides additional ideas for this pathway.

Suggestions for Storytelling with Families	
Backpack story pack	◆ A backpack story pack is a take-home tool designed to promote family involvement, offering children and their families easy, ready-to-use opportunities to engage in interactive reading and storytelling. ◆ The packs carry paper, pencils, crayons, tape, index cards, and books on various topics. The packs offer families activities to bring the story to life after reading the book, such as creating a poster on the topic, using the note cards to write learned facts about the topic, or drawing and discussing favorite parts of the book.
Family theme bags	◆ Family theme bags are like backpack story packs but venture across the curriculum. Create cloth bags representing a variety of themes for children to select, take home, and share with family members. ◆ Place handmade, theme-related puppets or stuffed animals in each bag, as well as creative fingerplay instructions, art supplies, trivia cards, and storybooks. ◆ Also provide a reflection journal so families can respond to the activities. • For example, in a zoo bag, suggest activities like playing animal-related games such as charades or watching animal films such as *March of the Penguins.*
Rotating resource library	◆ Make a diverse library of books, videos, and other resources available to families so they can check out materials and read them at home. ◆ Include parenting books on subjects such as positive reinforcement, sibling rivalry, bedtime routines, and nutrition. ◆ Offer helpful community brochures and web addresses for families to consult for support with a variety of issues.

Figure 10-3

Puppets as Pathways

When combined with other pathways, such as pantomime, storytelling, music and movement, and improvisation, puppets can help stakeholders gain a multidimensional picture of a child's inner world. They are a valuable tool to add to a prescriptive tool kit, particularly for helping children work on social skills—puppets serve a crucial curative role for children experiencing internalizing behaviors by permitting them to

Please consider . . .
Illustrated Storybooks

Beautifully illustrated storybooks are especially beneficial for children who are experiencing internalizing behaviors. Storybooks prompt discussions about situations that unfold in a child's life and help normalize adversity. Through them, children can learn to identify, understand, and cope with their emotions as well as relate to those of others. To visually enhance stories, add story aprons, puppets, or creative hand movements. For example, have children shake their hands like rustling leaves.

Books by Eric Carle are especially useful tools. Through beautiful illustrations, themes of nature, emotions, and friendship are expressed with creativity. Carle's books are supportive in increasing a child's emotional vocabulary, identifying emotional triggers, and learning ways to regulate feelings. These are some of his most popular books:

- *The Very Hungry Caterpillar*
- *The Very Quiet Cricket*
- *The Mixed-Up Chameleon*
- *The Very Clumsy Click Beetle*
- *The Very Lonely Firefly*
- *The Grouchy Ladybug*
- *The Very Busy Spider*

Handout 15: Literature to Develop Children's Social Skills

www.redleafpress.org
/tpp/h-15.pdf

Children learn and develop social skills effectively through beautifully illustrated literature that reinforces prosocial concepts. This handout outlines a variety of topics, as well as creative props, music, and movement to incorporate.

Music and Movement Pathways

- Children can gain insight about their own feelings and moods and that of others by listening to music and singing songs.
- Let children listen to various genres. While listening to different selections, have children express how the composer may have felt when the piece was written, such as sad, joyous, perky, shy, dreamy, or angry.
- Play background music, such as compositions by George Frideric Handel, Johann Sebastian Bach, or Wolfgang Amadeus Mozart, during arrival and departure times to help children transition, stay calm, and be productive.
- Select from a varied musical repertoire.
- Introduce a karaoke machine with a variety of musical selections for children to sing, move, and experience with props.
- For music and movement spaces, choose open, carpeted areas if possible. Use tumbling mats if carpeting is unavailable.
- Hang musical instruments on a pegboard and sort musical props into boxes.
- Keep the music and movement spaces organized and clutter-free.
- When possible, allow children to remove their shoes for freer movement.
- Set up a musical play space where children can listen to music individually. Provide adjustable headphones and an easy-to-use CD player.
- If possible, supply a record player so children can explore the sounds of old records.
- Music is also conducive to family involvement:
  - Families can learn to play a musical instrument, such as the recorder, together.
  - Through newsletters, invite families to attend community musical events, such as high school band performances, concerts, parades, festivals, and musical theaters.
- Allow children opportunities to tinker with an assortment of interesting musical instruments:
  - bongos
  - chimes
  - slide whistles
  - triangles
  - cymbals
  - wood blocks
  - rhythm sticks
  - shakers
  - improvised noisemakers, such as pots, pans, silverware, and wooden spoons
- Play pantomime games to music and use exaggerated body movements. For example, have children act out the following:
  - a rigid robot to reggae music
  - a slinky snake to a symphony
  - a jumbo jet to jazz music
- Provide props, such as movement scarves.

- Pantomime social behaviors:
  - receiving a gift to slow tempo music
  - playing tug-of-war to nature sounds
  - trying to open a window to sounds of Madam Butterfly
  - opening a stuck jar to *The Lone Ranger* theme song
- Use music and movement to broaden children's play experiences. For example:
  - Write in the air using large hand movements.
  - Clap rhythms and syllables.
  - Play Musical Tiptoes: Put colored mechanical tape or duct tape on the floor in a variety of designs, such as curvy, zigzag, parallel lines, or closed shapes. On the tiptoe tape, have children walk barefoot or in fuzzy socks.

Figure 10-4

Handout 16: Musical Selections for Children

Handout 17: Songs and Musical Instruments for Play

www.redleafpress.org
/tpp/h-16.pdf

www.redleafpress.org
/tpp/h-17.pdf

These handouts provide musical suggestions and simple and common songs to sing, say, or act out with puppets, story mitts, creative props, or as fingerplays.

rehearse more appropriate behaviors, scenarios, and conversations. Because children frequently project their thoughts and feelings onto puppets, puppets can support children in building their emotional language. In this way, they become safety objects and allow children the distance needed to communicate their distress.

Puppets also help bring a child's distress comfortably into their environment. For example, you can present circumstances in which the puppet has the same problem as the child and enlist in brainstorming solutions to solve the puppet's problem. Children frequently bond with their puppet friends and believe themselves their puppet's helper, which builds self-confidence.

Please consider . . .
The Power of Music

Music has the power to help children who are experiencing internalizing behaviors. It can relax muscles and soothe a child's anxious and depressed thoughts using several strategies:

- Mood Music (Goodyear-Brown 2010) is a beneficial technique that teaches children how to self-soothe while increasing their emotional language. The activity uses storytelling and musical instruments, such as a child-sized guitar.
- Let the child use headphones to listen to a relaxation CD with soothing sounds. If possible, let the child listen outdoors in a nature play space, as outlined on page 136. While there, encourage the child to listen for sounds of birds, insects, or wind.

For further study and strategies, refer to *Play Therapy with Traumatized Children: A Prescriptive Approach* by Paris Goodyear-Brown.

There are a variety of puppet types to choose from:

- sock puppets
- paper bag puppets
- hand puppets
- mitten puppets
- stick puppets
- dowel puppets
- finger puppets
- marionettes

An inexpensive idea to create puppetry is to remove the back (or bottom) stitching of plush stuffed animals and then take out a portion of the stuffing. Finger puppets made from felt are instant attention grabbers and add magic and drama to everyday activities and routines. Finger puppets can also be easily created from rubber balls by cutting a hole in the middle of the ball for a tiny index finger. Bring puppets to circle time to reenact and discuss situations.

Puppets as Pathways

- Make a puppet theater by setting up a simple box for an easy impromptu puppet show.
- Add sensory sock puppets—make sure different materials and textures are represented among the puppets you make available.
- Puppets that blink and give detailed facial expressions, such as those available from Puppets Inc., are excellent for children experiencing internalizing behaviors because they can more accurately represent emotions.
- Have children put personality into their hands with a puppet:
  - Make up wacky hand movements to funky music.
  - Pretend the puppet is nervous by having children shake their hands.
- Use videos or pictures to help children visualize impromptu objects, especially for cultural or geographical relevance.
  - For example, children in eastern states may not know how to pretend to be "a New Mexico tumbleweed blowing in the dusty wind."
- Use puppets and fingerplays to facilitate classroom transitions.
- Accompany sign language with puppets and creative props:
  - colorful streamers
  - handkerchiefs
  - bandannas
  - balloons
- Make a giant game board with sidewalk chalk. Have children and their puppets be the game pieces and move themselves around the board.
- Encourage conversation among puppets.
- Make exaggerated sounds and physical actions that children must imitate with their puppets.
- Do puppet interviews: Have children each make a paper bag puppet to represent themselves, then introduce their puppets and interview each other. Prompt children to ask questions such as "What is your name?" "What is your favorite color?" "What is something that makes you feel happy?" "What is something that makes you feel afraid?" "If you had three wishes, what would you wish for?" The puppets can be saved and used to help children solve later social issues that may present themselves.
- Play Pied Piper puppets using instrumental or flute music. Instruct children to follow an appointed child leader and imitate the moves and actions they make with their puppet.
- Teach prosocial behaviors by modeling a desired skill with a puppet while explaining how to properly carry it out. Puppets are useful while modeling because they allow for creative role playing.
- Lay out an oversized puzzle, scattering all its pieces on the floor. Using a puppet, model how to work as a team to clean up.

Figure 10-5

Please consider . . .
Creative Movement Brings Stories to Life

Show children how to use their bodies to improvise sounds and pantomime using creative and expressive movement to bring stories to life:

- slap knees
- tap feet
- hum
- pant
- snap their fingers
- click their tongues
- rub their hands back and forth
- growl
- grunt

Make improvised sounds:

- "ahhh"
- "shhhhhhhh"
- "whoooooosh"
- "bbbb"
- "kkkk"
- "st, st, st, st,"
- "sh, sh, sh, sh"
- "pop"

Make impromptu creative movements:

- sway
- glide
- make arcs above and around the body
- make whole-body waves
- roll
- skip
- tiptoe
- march
- clap
- pat

To connect to storytelling, create puppets for role playing so that children can dramatize and become the characters. Puppets can speak for children who are severely withdrawn, opening avenues of communication. In such cases, hide a puppet in a sack and encourage the child to coax the resistant puppet out by projecting the child's fears onto the puppet. Additional pathway ideas using puppets are presented in figure 10-5.

Please consider . . .
Miniature Play

The use of miniature play tools is beneficial in several ways for children experiencing internalizing behaviors:

- It naturally encourages self-reflection when children recreate characters and experiences through miniaturized scenes.
- It allows children to resolve conflict and remove obstacles within their dilemmas and gain self-acceptance of their difficulties.
- Dollhouses with tiny furniture and accessories, model trains, small figurines, and little cars and trucks are perfect for miniature fantasy play (see page 90).
- Tin soldiers and historical hero figurines can spark a child's creativity.
- Little lockboxes with secret keys or miniature household objects can catapult children into a world of make-believe.
- Small, soft blocks, petite lacing cubes, finger puppets, and music boxes are also perfect items for miniature play.

Sensory Pathways

Children struggling with internalizing behaviors often have different levels of physiological distress and dysregulation within their bodies. Sensory pathways, such as making wet and squishy mud pies, can help soothe a child's physiology and help them refocus while giving them words. It is important to provide children with pathways to express their feelings using sensory tools and experiences in a manner that is structured yet sensitive to any sensory challenges.

Sensory pathways such as water (clear, colored, scented) or sand (wet, dry, fine, coarse) invite children to expand their critical thinking and problem solving and relieve stress by engaging their senses. These pathways are beneficial because through them children learn emotional language and behavioral self-control as they practice responding appropriately to the stimulation provided. Sensory pathways can increase a child's ability to concentrate, reduce aggression, and improve social skills.

Sensory pathways should be made available indoors and outdoors and challenge as many of a child's senses as possible. They can be situated at a tub, bin, tray, or easel for one child or at a standing table big enough to accommodate several children. They can be filled with assorted substances like sand or sponges in different colors, textures, and sizes.

Sensory Pathways	
Clowning around	◆ Being sensitive to individual allergies (and fears), let children take turns using face paint to turn themselves into clowns. ◆ Use masking tape to create a tightrope for children to balance on. ◆ Have children paint with their toes using fingerpaint on newspaper spread on the floor. ◆ Offer a variety of paint textures and colors scented with interesting smells, such as lemon or vanilla extract.
Oobleck	◆ Read the Dr. Seuss book *Bartholomew and the Oobleck* as a class; then make oobleck and let children retell the tale with the gooey substance. ◆ Discuss how the oobleck feels, looks, smells, and changes in their hands. ◆ To vary sensory richness, freeze the oobleck for a melty and gooey experience, or make squishy sensory bags or discovery bottles. ◆ Offer children other substances, such as goop, Gak, gunk, and slime, for varied sensory play.
Bubble play	◆ Fill several big buckets and pots full of sudsy water. The more bubbles and foam the better. ◆ To increase sensory value with froth and fizz, add baking soda and vinegar. ◆ Add tools such as flyswatters and bubble wands of several sizes.
Fabulous fabrics	◆ Set up a sensory table with a patchwork of scrap fabric for children to sort through: • burlap • carpet chunks • corduroy • cotton balls • denim • fur • gauze • netting • silk • terry cloth • velvet • vinyl • wool ◆ Sprinkle fabrics with scents such as vanilla or lavender for richness. ◆ To extend fabric play, let children explore textures by sorting and classifying different kinds of soft, fuzzy, satiny, smooth, and coarse fabrics.

Sensory bins	◆ Sensory bins are hands-on tools for children to learn about their world using their senses. ◆ Sensory bins can calm, focus, and engage a child as well as help them build social skills. ◆ As children work with a variety of stimulating utensils such as wire whisks and interesting substances such as oobleck, they engage in conversation. Consider the following sensory bin ideas: • Messy boat bin (play with mini boats in Jell-O) • Box of buttons (find and sort different-sized and -colored buttons in sand)
Plasticine play	◆ Unlike playdough and clay, Plasticine stays soft, doesn't harden or dry, and won't stick to children's hands. ◆ Offer children modeling tools for shaping, sculpting, blending, texturing, thinning out, scraping, poking, and cutting Plasticine. ◆ Have children begin with flat sculptures and eventually move on to making complex objects. ◆ Add scented extracts, salt, or coffee grounds to Plasticine for increased texture and sensory value. ◆ Offer children a choice of sculpting bases (such as flat rocks, bricks, or cardboard) and sculpting tools (such as rolling pins, spoons, and spatulas). ◆ Show children how they can wind, bend, coil, fold, and wrap Plasticine to make three-dimensional shapes. ◆ Display books with illustrations using Plasticine figures, such as *New Baby Calf* by Edith Newlin Chase and *The Party* by Barbara Reid.
Mud murals	◆ Using clothesline play, as outlined on pages 141–42, drape old sheets over a clothesline for children to paint on with mud. ◆ Make use of big buckets to let children make a variety of textures. ◆ Mud can be made thicker with cornstarch, gritty with sand, or clumpy with petroleum gel.

Figure 10-6

Handout 18: Sensory Play Tools

www.redleafpress.org
/tpp/h-18.pdf

Sensory play and its tools are useful in calming children experiencing an internalizing behavior. This handout lists creative sensory play ideas and accompanying tools to enhance the richness of a child's sensory play. The resource also shares suggestions that encourage abstract thinking, experimentation, and safe storage.

Please consider . . .
Adding a Sensory Break Space

For children who are experiencing an internalizing behavior, a sensory break space is an area where they can go to gain individually needed sensory stimulation to calm down, wake up, stay alert, or refocus using various methods:

- doing wall pushups
- jumping into a mountain of soft pillows
- rocking in a chair with a weighted blanket on their lap
- playing with sand tables, playdough, or building blocks
- putting on a sleep mask and listening to quiet music in a small tent with an open flap
- eating a crunchy snack, such as carrots cut into coins

Color exploration is an effective sensory pathway where children can explore different hues, mix paints, look through kaleidoscopes, or safely dye fabrics. Add assorted accessories such as aprons with lots of pockets children can use to tote, store, and separate their tools as they play. Refer to figure 10-6 for further suggestions.

Pets

Children find emotional comfort sharing their experiences with animals through relationships with them. Montessori emphasized the importance of animals in a child's

Please consider . . .
Using Yoga

Yoga demands a child's full attention and is an effective relaxation strategy to help children calm their systems, particularly when combined with deep breathing, stretching, and reenacting poses. One of the most calming positions is called "child's pose," which shows children how to focus and self-regulate. There are many helpful videos on YouTube that demonstrate child's pose and other beginning yoga poses.

Ideas to pair yoga with other pathways include the following:

- Yoga can be combined with storytelling, games, or music and movement. For example, after a yoga session, read *Babar's Yoga for Elephants*, which takes children on Babar the elephant's playful yoga experience. Refer to Yogakids.com for further suggestions.
- Have children roll back and forth on a yoga ball, either in a seated position or on the stomach.
- *Yoga Pretzels* and *Body Poetry* yoga cards are useful calming activities for preschool programs. Visit Becker's School Supplies online for more information.

life and recommended creating a rich curriculum that includes children caring for animals. Relationships with animals have many benefits for a child, including providing social opportunities, supporting emotional regulation, offering companionship and nurturance during times of adversity, and increasing a child's sense of compassion, self-esteem, and responsibility.

Small and social rodents, such as gerbils and guinea pigs, work well for a child's environment. Goldfish or betta fish are also recommended, especially when children have allergies or are not developmentally ready to handle pets. A small aquarium adds richness to the setting with minimal maintenance yet emits a calm and comforting ambience.

Gardening

Gardening in fresh air and sunshine improves a child's emotional well-being and activates their creativity. The rhythmic nature of weeding and digging, combined with the sensation of preparing and feeling the texture of soil, helps children relax. Heavy "muscle" garden activities, such as hoeing, also promote the release of tension and reduce symptoms of depression. And, similar to caring for an animal, looking after a small section of blooming flowers or personal plot of seeded soil creates a connection that gives children a sense of responsibility and respect for living things. It improves their self-awareness and appreciation as they participate in the consistent nurturing and observation of the small details involved in gardening tasks—for example, becoming mindful not to step on budding sprouts. Gardening lets children become nurturers as they care for plants and witness the relationship between participating in that care, harvesting the results, building on what they have accomplished, having their efforts acknowledged, and sharing it with others.

Furthermore, children will enjoy planting a garden of bulbs, herbs, or veggies. Safe bulb choices include daffodils, tulips, and crocuses. Children can plant herb gardens according to themes, such as a spaghetti garden with parsley, oregano, and basil or a teatime garden with chamomile, lemon, spearmint, and peppermint. Give children their own garden space, even if that is only a small container or pot. Grow corn or start a pumpkin or strawberry patch. Use a trellis or other structure to grow beans, tomatoes, or sweet peas. Plant flowers that attract insects and birds near classroom windows. Situate a scarecrow within an outdoor garden. Hang bird feeders. Add a birdbath. Install a water feature, such as a simple fountain. Visit community gardens, children's farms, or botanic gardens for other ideas.

Cooking and Baking

Making food has therapeutic value to help ease internalizing behaviors. Like yoga, cooking is reflective and requires a child's entire attention. And like gardening, its repetitive actions, such as rolling and kneading dough with a heavy rolling pin, can have a calming and meditative impact on children. Cooking also permits many sensory experiences: the feel of flour, the whirl of a blender, the smell of ingredients and spices mixing in a big bowl. Cooking and baking can be modified according to a child's level of needed sensory stimulation and let children express their creativity. For example, cakes, cookies, and pancakes are blank canvases for children to paint on with frosting, maple syrup, honey, confectioners' sugar, cinnamon, fresh fruit, or softened butter.

Baking and cooking pathways are numerous and can be turned into creative play spaces within a child's indoor or outdoor environment. Outdoors, children can make mud pies and soups. Indoors, a bakery play space can be set up where children frost cupcakes, whisk instant pudding, or prepare no-bake cookies, simple snacks, and sandwiches. Creating people figures out of pretzel sticks and marshmallows is another simple yet creative activity to include at a bakery play space. Provide assorted baking and cooking utensils for children to work with, such as funnels, melon scoopers, frosting tubes, and pizza cutters.

Another idea: prepare several stacks of corn cakes (four inches in diameter work best) and provide an assortment of cookie cutters (not those used for playdough play). Let the child cut out patterns from the corn cakes. Add a few drops of food coloring to milk to use for paint. Use clean, small brushes to decorate the cutout cakes. If possible,

Please consider . . .
A Creative Bakery Play Space

A creative bakery play space can become an extension to a sensory break area.

- Working with chilled and scented bread dough can help children who need to calm down and release bottled-up energy. Have children put on an apron and "muscle" the dough:
  - squeeze it
  - spread it
  - squish it
  - pull it apart
  - pound it
  - mold it
  - twist it
  - poke it
  - smash it
  - roll it
- After muscling cookie or ceramic dough, lay out cookie cutters and let children create cookies or shapes to bake in an oven or kiln. Then paint.
- Use the play space for other food preparation activities, such as making mashed potatoes. Children will enjoy the entire process, from peeling the spuds to squashing them with potato mashers after cooking.

to enhance the activity socially, allow the child to assist in preparing the batter with a whisk and in flipping the corn cakes with supervision on a portable electric griddle.

◆◆◆◆◆

Playing out their emotions is much easier for children than discussing them. The pathways laid out in this chapter are natural modes of communication for children that are seldom resisted; they are self-expressive vehicles for the recovery process from internalizing behaviors. Use the suggestions presented here as is or as inspiration for children to jump-start their own pathway ideas. For the child who has experienced adversity or loss, pathways help to externalize the complexities of painful experiences, repressed memories, or unspoken fears, anxieties, or guilt.

Pathways allow a child's inner distress to surface, thus accelerating stakeholders' ability to proceed with EIIPS. They can provide useful information about a child's developmental levels and functioning. They also reveal unclear or inconsistent feelings and perceptions. Using creative pathways, stakeholders can break through resistive barriers and engage children while remembering to place emphasis on the pathway process and how the child can heal using it. Stakeholders are encouraged to be curious and learn as many pathways as possible to fill their prescriptive tool kits to support children with internalizing behaviors.

Conclusion

Throughout the process of writing this book, I explored accounts, read research, and reviewed resources regarding the increasing number of young children with unmet mental health needs. At times, frustration set in because I wondered how the very establishments created to deliver successful intervention services could have lost pace with the rising demands. Yet stakeholders are indeed developing focused efforts and partnerships to target key areas of concern. Several evolving projects and organizations, such as Parents for Children's Mental Health, are creating policy specific to childhood mental health challenges, reducing inconsistencies within those policies, and using evidenced-based practices to guide them. Such news is refreshing, as it is these early interactions between families and stakeholders that lay the groundwork for change.

Nevertheless, as all entities move forward, they must continue to gain knowledge of EIIPS and child development and stay abreast of an ever-evolving world that faces unprecedented new issues. (Pandemics, for instance.) With new challenges come additional childhood concerns that require support and efforts to prescriptively apply evidence-based, diverse, and individualized methods that best inform work with children.

Additionally, predicting the future of childhood mental wellness calls for deep exploration—exploration that serves as a strong foundation for a larger implementation plan for EIIPS as well as further time spent on specific areas such as creative pathways, attachment, symptomology, action signs, and more.

Ultimately, there are countless avenues to study, refine, and pursue avenues that have the potential to change the life trajectory of not only children who struggle with internalizing behaviors but those who have committed their own lives to caring for them.

Helpful Handouts

To help you get started, I have created a series of handouts meant to complement the cathartic powers of play and its tools, support children experiencing an internalizing behavior, encourage family involvement, and enhance their unique formulas. These handouts are designed to assist stakeholders, children, and their families with a variety of issues, including emotional regulation, social skills, and effective communication. Also included are listings of suggested music, movement, and visual art activities and creative tools. Other perks of the section include a useful page to fill out when preparing for an appointment with a child's pediatrician or teacher, as well as a convenient family questionnaire to gather information about a child's home environment and culture. Added resources and references are also listed on each handout for further study on the topic.

The handouts are practical advice meant to be shared with families and stakeholders working with children experiencing internalizing behaviors. Each handout encourages supportive conversations with families about their children's mental wellness and overall development and were designed to be individually adapted for children.

Handout 1: Child Temperament and Goodness of Fit
www.redleafpress.org/tpp/h-1.pdf

Handout 2: Child Temperament Scale
www.redleafpress.org/tpp/h-2.pdf

Handout 3: Multiple Intelligences and Learning Styles
www.redleafpress.org/tpp/h-3.pdf

Handout 4: Sample Family Questionnaire
www.redleafpress.org/tpp/h-4.pdf

Handout 5: Effective Family Communications
www.redleafpress.org/tpp/h-5.pdf

Handout 6: Understanding Adverse Childhood Experiences
www.redleafpress.org/tpp/h-6.pdf

Handout 7: Preparing for an Appointment
www.redleafpress.org/tpp/h-7.pdf

Handout 8: Strategies to Develop a Child's Emotional Regulation
www.redleafpress.org/tpp/h-8.pdf

Handout 9: Fostering Intrinsic Motivation
www.redleafpress.org/tpp/h-9.pdf

Handout 10: Creative Movement Ideas
www.redleafpress.org/tpp/h-10.pdf

Handout 11: Transitioning Ideas
www.redleafpress.org/tpp/h-11.pdf

Handout 12: Instructional Strategies
www.redleafpress.org/tpp/h-12.pdf

Handout 13: The Importance of Family Involvement
www.redleafpress.org/tpp/h-13.pdf

Handout 14: Tools for Play Spaces, Creative Pathways, and Self-Expression
www.redleafpress.org/tpp/h-14.pdf

Handout 15: Literature to Develop Children's Social Skills
www.redleafpress.org/tpp/h-15.pdf

Handout 16: Musical Selections for Children
www.redleafpress.org/tpp/h-16.pdf

Handout 17: Songs and Musical Instruments for Play
www.redleafpress.org/tpp/h-17.pdf

Handout 18: Sensory Play Tools
www.redleafpress.org/tpp/h-18.pdf

References

Acar, Habibe. 2014. "Learning Environments for Children in Outdoor Spaces." *Procedia—Social and Behavioral Sciences* 141 (August): 846–53. https://doi.org/10.1016/j.sbspro.2014.05.147.

American Academy of Neurology. 2015. "Can Arts, Crafts and Computer Use Preserve Your Memory?" Press release, April 8, 2015. https://www.aan.com/PressRoom/Home/PressRelease/1363.

American Psychiatric Association. 2013. *Diagnostic and Statistical Manual of Mental Disorders (DSM-5)*. Washington, DC: American Psychiatric Association.

And Next Comes L: Your Go-To Resource for Hyperlexia. n.d. Accessed October 6, 2020. www.andnextcomesl.com.

Armstrong, Thomas. 1987. *In Their Own Way, Discovering and Encouraging Your Child's Multiple Intelligences*. Los Angeles: Jeremy P. Tarcher.

Axline, Virginia Mae. 1947. *Play Therapy: The Inner Dynamics of Childhood*. Edited by Leonard Carmichael. Boston: Houghton Mifflin.

Azlina, Wan, and A. S. Zulkiflee. 2012. "A Pilot Study: The Impact of Outdoor Play Spaces on Kindergarten Children." *Procedia-Social and Behavioral Sciences* 38:275–83. https://doi.org/10.1016/j.sbspro.2012.03.349.

Bailey, Rebecca Anne. 1997. *There's Gotta Be a Better Way: Discipline That Works!* Oviedo, FL: Loving Guidance.

Bayat, Mojdeh. 2019. *Addressing Challenging Behaviors and Mental Health Issues in Early Childhood*. New York: Routledge.

Benham, Anne Leland, and Carol Fisher Slotnick. 2006. "Play Therapy: Integrating Clinical and Developmental Perspectives." In *Handbook of Preschool Mental Health: Development, Disorders, and Treatment*, edited by Joan L. Luby, 331–71. New York: Guilford Press.

Berger, Rebecca H., Alison L. Miller, Ronald Seifer, Stephanie R. Cares, Monique K. LeBourgeois. 2012. "Acute Sleep Restriction Effects on Emotion Responses in 30- to 36-Month-Old Children." *Journal of Sleep Research* 21 (3): 235–46. https://doi.org/10.1111/j.1365-2869.2011.00962.x.

Biddle, Kimberly. 2018. "Childhood Depression: Symptoms and Treatment Moria Jackson moria_jackson@ hotmail.com Social/Emotional Development–CHDV 138."

Biederman, Joseph, Jerrold F. Rosenbaum, Elizabeth A. Bolduc-Murphy, Stephen V. Faraone, Jonathan Chaloff, Dina R. Hirshfeld, and Jerome Kagan. 1993. "A 3-Year Follow-Up of Children with and without Behavioral Inhibition." *Journal of the American Academy of Child & Adolescent Psychiatry* 32 (4): 814–21. https://doi.org/10.1097/00004583-199307000-00016.

Biel, Lindsey. 2017. "Students with Sensory Processing Challenges: Classroom Strategies." In *Optimizing Learning Outcomes: Proven Brain-Centric, Trauma-Sensitive Practices*, edited by William Steele, 90–110. New York: Routledge.

Biel, Lindsey, and Nancy K. Peske. 2005. *Raising a Sensory Smart Child: The Definitive Handbook for Helping Your Child with Sensory Integration Issues*. New York: Penguin.

Bitonte, Robert A., and Marisa De Santo. 2014. "Art Therapy: An Underutilized, yet Effective Tool." *Mental Illness* 6, no. 1 (March 4): 5354. https://doi.org/10.4081/mi.2014.5354.

Black, Maureen M., Susan P. Walker, Lia C. H. Fernald, Christopher T. Andersen, Ann M. DiGirolamo, Chunling Lu, Dana C. McCoy, Günther Fink, Yusra R. Shawar, Jeremy Shiffman, Amanda E. Devercelli, Quentin T. Wodon, Emily Vargas-Barón, Sally Grantham-McGregor. 2017. "Early Childhood Development Coming of Age: Science through the Life Course." *Lancet* 389, no. 10064 (January 7): 77–90. https://doi.org/10.1016/S0140-6736(16)31389-7.

Bolwerk Anne, Jessica Mack-Andrick, Frieder R. Lang, Arnd Dörfler, Christian Maihöfner. 2014. "How Art Changes Your Brain: Differential Effects of Visual Art Production and Cognitive Art Evaluation on Functional Brain Connectivity." *PLoS ONE* 9, no. 7 (July 1): e101035. https://doi.org/10.1371/journal.pone.0101035.

Bos, Candace S., and Sharon Vaughn. 1994. *Strategies for Teaching Students with Learning and Behavior Problems*. Boston: Allyn and Bacon.

Bowen, J., William R. Jensen, and Elaine Clark. 2004. *School-Based Interventions for Students with Behavior Problems*. New York: Springer Science+Business Media.

Bowker, Michele. 2020. "Benefits of Incorporating Howard Gardner's Multiple Intelligences Theory into Teaching Practices." MS thesis, California State University, Monterey Bay: Digital Commons @ CSUMB.

Brauner, Cheryl Boydell, and Cheryll Bowers Stephens. 2006. "Estimating the Prevalence of Early Childhood Serious Emotional/Behavioral Disorders: Challenges and Recommendations." *Public Health Reports* 121, no. 3 (May–June): 303–10. https://doi.org/10.1177/003335490612100314.

Bricker, Diane, Maura Schoen Davis, and Jane Squires. 2004. "Mental Health Screening in Young Children." *Infants & Young Children* 17, no. 2 (April): 129–44.

Briefel, Ronette R., Denise M. Deming, and Kathleen C. Reidy. 2015. "Peer Reviewed: Parents' Perceptions and Adherence to Children's Diet and Activity Recommendations: The 2008 Feeding Infants and Toddlers Study." *Preventing Chronic Disease* 12 (September 24). https://doi.org/10.5888/pcd12.150110.

Bromfield, Richard N. 2003. "Psychoanalytic Play Therapy." In *Foundations of Play Therapy,* edited by Charles E. Schaefer, 1–13. Hoboken, NJ: John Wiley and Sons.

Bronson, Martha. 2000. *Self-Regulation in Early Childhood: Nature and Nurture.* New York: Guilford Press.

Brown, Stuart. 2014. "Play, Spirit, and Character." https://soundcloud.com/onbeing/sets/stuart-brown-play-spirit-and.

Bruer, John T. 2015. "Windows of Opportunity: Their Seductive Appeal." *Evidence Speaks Reports* 1, no. 5.

Bufferd, Sara J., Lea R. Dougherty, Gabrielle A. Carlson, and Daniel N. Klein. 2011. "Parent-Reported Mental Health in Preschoolers: Findings Using a Diagnostic Interview." *Comprehensive Psychiatry* 52, no. 4 (July–August): 359–69.

Bufferd, Sara J., Lea R. Dougherty, Gabrielle A. Carlson, Suzanne Rose, and Daniel N. Klein. 2012. "Psychiatric Disorders in Preschoolers: Continuity from Ages 3 to 6." *American Journal of Psychiatry* 169, no. 11 (November):1157–64.

Butin, D. 2000. National Institute of Building Sciences Thomas Jefferson Center for Educational Design, University of Virginia, 1–4.

Carpenter, Aubrey L., Anthony C. Puliafico, Steven M. S. Kurtz, Donna B. Pincus, and Jonathan S. Comer. 2014. "Extending Parent–Child Interaction Therapy for Early Childhood Internalizing Problems: New Advances for an Overlooked Population." *Clinical Child and Family Psychology Review* 17, no. 4 (December): 340–56. https://doi.org/10.1007/s10567-014-0172-4.

Carpenter, Kimberly L. H., Pablo Sprechmann, Robert Calderbank, Guillermo Sapiro, and Helen L. Egger. 2016. "Quantifying Risk for Anxiety Disorders in Preschool Children: A Machine Learning Approach." *PloS One* 11, no. 11 (November): e0165524. https://doi.org/10.1371/journal.pone.0165524.

Centers for Disease Control and Prevention. 2017. "Family Health History and Diabetes." Page last reviewed Oct. 23, 2020. www.cdc.gov/features/family-history-diabetes/index.html.

Chess, Stella, and Alexander Thomas. 1977. "Temperamental Individuality from Childhood to Adolescence." *Journal of Child Psychiatry,* 16, no. 2 (March): 218–26. https://doi.org/10.1016/s0002-7138(09)60038-8.

———. 1991. "Temperament and the Concept of Goodness of Fit." In *Explorations in Temperament: International Perspectives on Theory and Measurement,* edited by Jan Strelau and Alois Angleitner, 15–28. Boston: Springer. https://doi.org/10.1007/978-1-4899-0643-4_2.

Clark, Heather R., Elizabeth Goyder, Paul Bissell, Lindsay Blank, and Jean Peters. 2007. "How Do Parents' Child-Feeding Behaviours Influence Child Weight? Implications for Childhood Obesity Policy." *Journal of Public Health* 29, no. 2 (April 18): 132–41. https://doi.org/10.1093/pubmed/fdm012.

Chronis-Tuscano, Andrea, Christina M. Danko, Kenneth H. Rubin, Robert J. Coplan, and Danielle R. Novick. 2018. "Future Directions for Research on Early Intervention for Young Children at Risk for Social Anxiety." *Journal of Clinical Child & Adolescent Psychology* (July–August): 1–13.

Coates, Annette, Barbara Bigelow, Bobbi-Lynn Keating, and Carol Anne Wien. 2008. "Moving into Uncertainty: Sculpture with Three-to-Five-Year-Olds." *Young Children* 63, no. 4 (January): 78–86.

Cohen, Stewart, and Susan L. Trostle. 1990. "Young Children's Preferences for School-Related Physical-Environmental Setting Characteristics." *Environment and Behavior* 22 (6): 753–66. https://doi.org/10.1177/0013916590226002.

Crain, William. 1997. "How Nature Helps Children Develop." *Montessori Life* 9, no. 2 (Spring): 41–43.

Csikszentmihalyi, Mihaly. 2008. *Flow: The Psychology of Optimal Experience.* New York: HarperCollins.

Dancer, Ashlea. 2012. "Pets in the Classroom: The Difference They Can Make." MS thesis, St. John Fisher College, Rochester, NY: Fisher Digital Publications.

Danoff-Burg, James A. 2002. "Be a Bee and Other Approaches to Introducing Young Children to Entomology." *Young Children* 57, no. 5 (September): 42–46.

Davies, Douglas. 2010. *Child Development: A Practitioner's Guide.* 3rd ed. New York: Guilford Press.

Deci, Edward L. 1975. *Intrinsic Motivation.* New York: Plenum.

Deci, Edward L., and Richard M. Ryan, 1985. *Intrinsic Motivation and Self-Determination in Human Behavior.* New York: Plenum.

Degges-White, S. 2020. "Expressive Arts in Schools: Visual and Performing Arts and Sandtray Interventions to Promote Self-Discovery." In *Applying Psychology in the Schools. Promoting Mind-Body Health in Schools: Interventions for Mental Health Professionals,* edited by C. Maykel and M. A. Bray, 217–32. American Psychological Association. https://doi.org/10.1037/0000157-015.

DeLoatche, Kendall Jeffries, Kathy L. Bradley-Klug, Julia Ogg, Jeffrey D. Kromrey, and Ashley N. Sundman-Wheat. 2015. "Increasing Parent Involvement among Head Start Families: A Randomized Control Group Study." *Early Childhood Education Journal* 43, no. 4 (July): 271–79.

Denham, Susanne A., and Rosemary Burton. 2003. *Social and Emotional Prevention and Intervention Programming for Preschoolers.* New York: Kluwer Academic/Plenum.

Dr. Seuss. 1971. *The Lorax.* New York: Random House Books for Young Readers.

Dodge, Diane Trister, Laura Colker, and Cate Heroman. 2002. *The Creative Curriculum for Preschool,* 4th ed. Washington, DC: Teaching Strategies.

Donison, Laurel. 2018. "Young Children's Preferences of the Elements Available to Them in Their Outdoor Play Space." PhD diss., University of British Columbia.

Dougherty, Lea R., Katherine A. Leppert, Stephanie M. Merwin, Victoria C. Smith, Sara J. Bufferd, and Marissa R. Kushner. 2015. "Advances and Directions in Preschool Mental Health Research." *Child Development Perspectives* 9, no. 1 (January 9): 14–19. https://doi.org/10.1111/cdep.12099.

Douglass, Frederick. 1855. *My Bondage, My Freedom*. Urbana and Chicago: University of Illinois Press.

Downing, Katherine L., Trina Hinkley, Jo Salmon, Jill A. Hnatiuk, and Kylie D. Hesketh. 2017. "Do the Correlates of Screen Time and Sedentary Time Differ in Preschool Children?" *BMC Public Health* 17 (1): 285.

Duncan, Sandra, Jody Martin, and Sally Haughey. 2018. *Through a Child's Eyes*. www.kaplanco.com/SenseOfPlace.

Dunlop, William L., and Mark R. Beauchamp. 2012. "The Relationship between Intra-Group Age Similarity and Exercise Adherence." *American Journal of Preventive Medicine* 42, no. 1 (January): 53–55. https://doi.org/10.1016/j.amepre.2011.08.018.

Dunn, Winnie. 1997. "The Impact of Sensory Processing Abilities on the Daily Lives of Young Children and Their Families: A Conceptual Model." *Infants and Young Children* 9, no. 4 (April): 23–35.

Ebbeling, Cara B., Dorota B. Pawlak, and David S. Ludwig. 2002. "Childhood Obesity: Public-Health Crisis, Common Sense Cure." *Lancet* 360, no. 9331 (August 10): 473–82. https://doi.org/10.1016/S0140-6736(02)09678-2.

Eisen, George. 1988. *Children and Play in the Holocaust*. Amherst: University of Massachusetts Press.

Elliot, Mary Jane. 1998. "Great Moments of Learning in Project Work." *Young Children* 53 no. 4 (July): 55–59.

Elmacı, Dilek Tunçay, and Sibel Cevizci. 2015. "Dog-Assisted Therapies and Activities in Rehabilitation of Children with Cerebral Palsy and Physical and Mental Disabilities." *International Journal of Environmental Research and Public Health* 12, no. 5 (May 12): 5046–60. https://doi.org/10.3390/ijerph120505046.

Epstein, Joyce L., and Karen Clark Salinas. 2004. "Partnering with Families and Communities." *Educational Leadership* 61, no. 8 (May): 12–19.

Erikson, Erik H. 1950. *Childhood and Society*. New York: W. W. Norton & Company.

Ernst, J., M. Johnson, and F. Burcak. 2019. "The Nature and Nurture of Resilience: Exploring the Impact of Nature Preschools on Young Children's Protective Factors." *International Journal of Early Childhood Environmental Education* 6 (2): 7–18.

Feitelson, Dina, and Gail S. Ross. 1973. "The Neglected Factor–Play." *Human Development* 16 (3): 202–23.

Fernandez, Karina Therese G., and Celine O. Sugay. 2016. "Psychodynamic Play Therapy: A Case of Selective Mutism." *International Journal of Play Therapy* 25 (4): 203–9. https://doi.org/10.1037/pla0000034.

Firlik, Russ. 1997. "Designing New Schools: The Race for Space." *Principal* 75, no. 4 (March) 38–41.

Frailberg, Selma H. 1951. "Clinical Notes on the Nature of Transference in Child Analysis," *The Psychoanalytic Study of the Child* 6(1): 286–306, DOI: 10.1080/00797308.1952.11822917.Frank, Lawrence. K. 1948. *Projective Methods*. Springfield, IL: Charles C. Thomas.

Franz, Lauren, Adrian Angold, William Copeland, E. Jane Costello, Nissa Towe-Goodman, and Helen Egger. 2013. "Preschool Anxiety Disorders in Pediatric Primary Care: Prevalence and Comorbidity." *Journal of the American Academy of Child & Adolescent Psychiatry* 52, no. 12 (September 27): 1294–1303. https://doi.org/10.1016/j.jaac.2013.09.008.

Freud, Sigmund. (1912) 1958. "The Dynamics of Transference." In *The Standard Edition of the Complete Psychological Works of Sigmund Freud*, vol. 12, edited by J. Strachey. London: Hogarth.

Froebel, Friedrich. 1887. *The Education of Man*. New York and London: D. Appleton and Company.

Froebel Web. n.d. "Friedrich Froebel Created Kindergarten." Accessed November 29. www.froebelweb.org.

Frostig, Marianne. 1970. *Movement Education: Theory and Practice*. Chicago: Follett Educational Corporation.

Fuller, Buckminster. 1972. *Buckminster Fuller to Children of Earth*. Compiled and photographed by Cam Smith. New York: Doubleday.

Ganz, J. B., and Margaret M. Flores. 2010. "Implementing Visual Cues for Young Children with Autism Spectrum Disorders and Their Classmates." *Young Children* 65, no. 3 (February): 78–83.

Gardner, Howard. 1983. *Frames of Mind*. New York: Basic Books.

———. 1996. "Multiple Intelligences." In *Developing Museum Exhibitions for Lifelong Learning*, edited by Gail Durbin, 8. Museums and Galleries Commission. London: The Stationery Office.

Gariépy, Nadine, and Nina Howe. 2003. "The Therapeutic Power of Play: Examining the Play of Young Children with Leukaemia." *Child: Care, Health and Development* 29, no. 6 (December): 523–37. https://doi.org/10.1046/j.1365-2214.2003.00372.x.

Gehris, J. S., R. A. Gooze, and R. C. Whitaker. 2015. "Teachers' Perceptions about Children's Movement and Learning in Early Childhood Education Programs." *Child: Care, Health and Development* 41, no. 1 (January): 122–31. https://doi.org/10.1111/cch.12136.

Giles, Martha Mead. 1991. "A Little Background Music, Please." *Principal* 71 (2): 41–44.

Ginsburg, Kenneth R. 2007. "The Importance of Play in Promoting Healthy Child Development and Maintaining Strong Parent-Child Bonds." *Pediatrics* 119, no. 1 (January): 182–91. https://doi.org/10.1542/peds.2006-2697.

Goertzel, Victor, and Mildred Geore Goertzel. 1962. *Cradles of Eminence.* Boston: Little, Brown and Company.

Goldfield, Gary S., Alysha Harvey, Kimberly Grattan, and Kristi B. Adamo. 2012. "Physical Activity Promotion in the Preschool Years: A Critical Period to Intervene." *International Journal of Environmental Research and Public Health* 9, no. 4 (April 16): 1326–42. https://doi.org/10.3390/ijerph9041326.

Goldings, Carmen R., and Herbert J. Goldings. 1972. "Books in the Playroom: A Dimension of Child Psychiatric Technique." *Journal of the American Academy of Child Psychiatry* 11 (1): 52–65. https://doi.org/10.1016/S0002-7138(09)61804-5.

Goldstein, Jeffrey. 2003. "Contributions of Play and Toys to Child Development." Brussels: Toy Industries of Europe.

Goodyear-Brown, Paris. 2010. *Play Therapy with Traumatized Children: A Prescriptive Approach.* Hoboken, NJ: John Wiley and Sons.

Göttken, Tanja, Lars O. White, Annette M. Klein, and Kai von Klitzing. 2014. "Short-Term Psychoanalytic Child Therapy for Anxious Children: A Pilot Study." *Psychotherapy* 51, no. 1 (March): 148–58. https://doi.org/10.1037/a0036026.

Gray, Peter. 2011. "The Decline of Play and the Rise of Psychopathology in Children and Adolescents." *American Journal of Play* 3:443-63.

Green, Edward, Paul F. Cook, and Lorraine Bolt. 1996. "Fitting New Technologies into Traditional Classrooms: Two Case Studies in the Design of Improved Learning Facilities." *Educational Technology* (July–August): 27–38.

Greenman, Jim. 1988. *Caring Spaces, Learning Places: Children's Environments That Work.* Redmond, WA: Exchange Press.

Gruber, R. 2015. "Sleep and Children: The Impact of Lack of Sleep on Daily Life." Montreal: Douglas Mental Health University Institute.

Halfon, Sibel, Alev Çavdar, Franco Orsucci, Gunter K. Schiepek, Silvia Andreassi, Alessandro Giuliani, and Giulio de Felice. 2016. "The Non-linear Trajectory of Change in Play Profiles of Three Children in Psychodynamic Play Therapy." *Frontiers in Psychology* 7 (2016): 1494.

Hannaford, Carla. 1995. *Smart Moves: Why Learning Is Not All in Your Head.* Arlington, VA: Great Ocean.

Harvey, Margarete R. 1989. "Children's Experiences with Vegetation on School Grounds. Their Botanical Knowledge and Environmental Dispositions." Environmental Design Association.

Herrington, Susan, and Ken Studtmann. 1998. "Landscape Interventions: New Directions for the Design of Children's Outdoor Play Environments." *Landscape and Urban Planning* 42, no. 2–4 (December): 191–205. https://doi.org/10.1016/S0169-2046(98)00087-5.

Hinkley, Trina, David Crawford, Jo Salmon, Anthony D. Okely, and Kylie Hesketh. 2008. "Preschool Children and Physical Activity: A Review of Correlates." *American Journal of Preventive Medicine* 34, no. 5 (May): 435–41. https://doi.org/10.1016/j.amepre.2008.02.001.

Hodgdon, Linda A. 1995. *Visual Strategies for Improving Communication. Vol. 1: Practical Supports for School and Home.* Troy, MI: QuirkRoberts.

Hodgkin, Robin A. 1976. *Born Curious: New Perspectives in Educational Theory.* Hoboken, NJ: John Wiley and Sons, 1976.

Hodgkinson, Stacy, Leandra Godoy, Lee Savio Beers, and Amy Lewin. 2017. "Improving Mental Health Access for Low-Income Children and Families in the Primary Care Setting." *Pediatrics* 139, no. 1.

Holley, Cynthia, and Jane Walkup. 1993. *First Time, Circle Time.* Parsippany, NJ: Fearon Teacher Aids.

Holmes, Cheryl, Michelle Levy, Avis Smith, Susan Pinne, and Paula Neese. 2015. "A Model for Creating a Supportive Trauma-Informed Culture for Children in Preschool Settings." *Journal of Child and Family Studies* 24 (6): 1650–59. https://doi.org/10.1007/s10826-014-9968-6.

Homburger, Erik. 1937. "Configurations in Play—Clinical Notes." *Psychoanalytic Quarterly* 6 (2):139–214. https://doi.org/10.1080/21674086.1937.11925315.

Howell, Jacky, and Lynn Corbey-Scullen. 1997. "Out of the Housekeeping Corner and onto the Stage—Extending Dramatic Play." *Young Children* 52 (6): 82–88.

Hudziak, Jim, and Christopher Archangeli. 2017. "The Future of Preschool Prevention, Assessment, and Intervention." *Child and Adolescent Psychiatric Clinics* 26, no. 3 (July 1): 611–24.

Huizinga, Johan. 1955. *Homo Ludens: A Study of the Play Element in Culture.* London: Routledge & Keegan Paul: 446.

Illinois Facilities Fund. 2000. "Great Spaces, Fresh Places: How to Improve Environments for School-Age Programs."

Isbell, Rebecca, and Betty Exelby. 2001. *Early Learning Environments That Work.* Silver Spring, MD: Gryphon House.

Ingersoll, Barbara, Sam Goldstein, and Pamela Ramser. 1996. *Lonely, Sad, and Angry: A Parent's Guide to Depression in Children and Adolescents.* New York: Doubleday.

Intro to Psychology: Help and Review Course. 2015. "Internalizing Behaviors: Definition & Examples." Study.com. Accessed June 24, 2018. https://study.com/academy/lesson/internalizing-behaviors-definition-examples-quiz.html.

Jacobson, Nora, and Dianne Greenley. 2001. "A Conceptual Model of Recovery." Letter to the editor. *Psychiatric Services* 52, no. 5 (May 1): 688.

Jensen, Eric. 2006. "Principles of Brain-Based Learning." Jensen Learning. http://www.jensenlearning.com/principles.php.

Jensen, Peter S., Eliot Goldman, David Offord, Elizabeth J. Costello, Robert Friedman, Barbara Huff, Maura Crowe, Lawrence Amsel, Kathryn Bennett, Hector Bird, Rand Conger, Prudence Fisher, Kimberly Hoagwood, Ronald C. Kessler, and Robert Roberts. 2011. "Overlooked and Underserved: 'Action Signs' for Identifying Children with Unmet Mental Health Needs." *Pediatrics* 128, no. 5 (November): 970–79.

Jones, Nancy P. 2005. "Big Jobs: Planning for Competence." *Young Children* 60, no. 2 (March): 86–93.

Kaduson, Heidi, and Donna M. Cangelosi, eds. 1997. *The Playing Cure: Individualized Play Therapy for Specific Childhood Problems*. Northvale, NJ: Jason Aronson.

Keeler, Rusty. 2003. "Designing and Creating Natural Play Environments for Young Children." *Child Care Information Exchange* 150: 43–45.

———. 2008. *Natural Playscapes: Creating Outdoor Play Environments for the Soul*. Redmond, WA: Exchange Press.

Kendall-Taylor, Nat, and Anna Mikulak. 2009. *Child Mental Health: A Review of the Scientific Discourse*. Washington, DC: FrameWorks Institute.

Kidd, Sunnie D. n.d. "On Poetic Imagination: Sigmund Freud and Martin Heidegger." *InBetweenness*. PDF file.

Kinnell, Gretchen. 2009. *Why Children Bite: A Family Companion to "No Biting."* St. Paul, MN: Redleaf Press.

Kinsner, Kathy. 2019. "Fresh Air, Fun, and Exploration: Why Outdoor Play Is Essential for Healthy Development." *Young Children* 74 (2): 90–92.

Klein, Melanie. 1955. "The Psychoanalytic Play Technique." *American Journal of Orthopsychiatry* 25, no. 2 (April): 223–37. https://doi.org/10.1111/j.1939-0025.1955.tb00131.x.

Klein, S. 2011. "Creating Cozy, Comfy, and Cuddly Childcare," 1–3. Community Playthings. www.communityplaythings.com/resources/articles/2008/creating-cozy--comfy--and-cuddly-childcare.

Kluckhohn, Clyde, and Henry A. Murray. 1953. *Personality in Nature, Society, and Culture*. 2nd ed. New York: Knopf.

Knight, Zelda Gillian. 2017. "A Proposed Model of Psychodynamic Psychotherapy Linked to Erik Erikson's Eight Stages of Psychosocial Development." *Clinical Psychology & Psychotherapy* 24 (5): 1047–58.

Koplewicz, Harold S., and Robin F. Goodman, eds. 1999. *Childhood Revealed: Art Expressing Pain, Discovery & Hope*. New York: Harry N. Abrams.

Kostelnik, Marjorie J. 1993. "Recognizing the Essentials of Developmentally Appropriate Practice." *Child Care Information Exchange* 90, no. 3 (March–April): 73–77.

Kottman, Terry, and Charles Schaefer, eds. 1994. *Play Therapy in Action: A Casebook for Practitioners*. Lanham, MD: Jason Aronson.

Kranowitz, Carol Stock. 2005. *The Out-of-Sync Child: Recognizing and Coping with Sensory Processing Disorder*. New York: Tarcher Perigee.

Kurdziel, Laura, Kasey Duclos, and Rebecca M. C. Spencer. 2013. "Sleep Spindles in Midday Naps Enhance Learning in Preschool Children." *Proceedings of the National Academy of Sciences* (epub ahead of print). https://doi.org/10.1073/pnas.1306418110.

Lackney, Jeffery. 1998. "12 Design Principles Based on Brain-Based Learning Research." Indus Training and Research Institute, 1–5.

Lamm, Sandra, Judith G. Groulx, Cindy Hansen, Mary Martin Patton, and Anna Jimenez Slaton. 2006. "Creating Environments for Peaceful Problem Solving." *Young Children* 61 (6): 22–28.

Landreth, G. L. 1993. "Self-Expressive Communication." In *The Therapeutic Powers of Play*, edited by C. E. Schaefer, 41–63. Northvale, NJ: Jason Aronson.

Larouche, Richard, Didier Garriguet, Katie E. Gunnell, Gary S. Goldfield, and Mark S. Tremblay. 2016. *Outdoor Time, Physical Activity, Sedentary Time, and Health Indicators at Ages 7 to 14: 2012/2013 Canadian Health Measures Survey*. Statistics Canada.

Lecompte, Vanessa, Ellen Moss, Chantal Cyr, and Katherine Pascuzzo. 2014. "Preschool Attachment, Self-Esteem and the Development of Preadolescent Anxiety and Depressive Symptoms." *Attachment & Human Development* 16 (3): 242–60.

Lentini, Rochelle, Bobbie J. Vaughn, and Lise Fox. 2004. "Routine-Based Support Guide for Young Children with Challenging Behavior." Tampa: University of South Florida, Early Intervention Behavior Support.

Lieberman, J. Nina. 1965. "Playfulness and Divergent Thinking: An Investigation of Their Relationship at the Kindergarten Level." *Journal of Genetic Psychology* 107 (2): 219–24. https://doi.org/10.1080/00221325.1965.10533661.

Lipsky, Rebecca. 2020. "Using Plasticity in the Treatment of Children with Depression." PhD diss., Stern College for Women. Yeshiva University New York.

Liu, Jia Jia, Yanping Bao, Xiaolin Huang, Jie Shi, and Lin Lu. 2020. "Mental Health Considerations for Children Quarantined Because of COVID-19." *Lancet Child & Adolescent Health* 4, no. 5 (May): 347–49. https://doi.org/10.1016/S2352-4642(20)30096-1.

Lopresti, Adrian L. 2015. "A Review of Nutrient Treatments for Pediatric Depression." *Journal of Affective Disorders* 181 (August 1): 24–32.

Louv, Richard. 1991. *Childhood's Future.* New York: Doubleday.

———. 2008. *Last Child in the Woods: Saving Our Children from Nature-Deficit Disorder.* Chapel Hill, NC: Algonquin Books.

Luby, Joan L., ed. 2009. *Handbook of Preschool Mental Health: Development, Disorders, and Treatment.* New York: Guilford Press.

———. 2012. "Dispelling the 'They'll Grow Out of It' Myth: Implications for Intervention." *American Journal of Psychiatry* 169, no. 11 (November 1): 1127–29.

Luby, Joan L., A. K. Heffelfinger, C. Mrakotsky, K. M. Brown, M. J. Hessler, J. M. Wallis, and E. L. Spitznagel. 2003. "The Clinical Picture of Depression in Preschool Children." *Journal of the American Academy of Child & Adolescent Psychiatry* 42 (3): 340–48. https://doi.org/10.1097/00004583-200303000-00015.

Luby, Joan, Shannon Lenze, and Rebecca Tillman. 2012. "A Novel Early Intervention for Preschool Depression: Findings from a Pilot Randomized Controlled Trial." *Journal of Child Psychology and Psychiatry* 53, no. 3 (March): 313–22. https://doi.org/10.1111/j.1469-7610.2011.02483.x.

Luby, Joan L., Diana Whalen, and C. H. Zeanah. 2018. "Depression in Early Childhood." *Handbook of Infant Mental Health*, 4th ed., edited by Charles H. Zeanah. New York: Guilford Press.

Lumeng, Julie C., Deepak Somashekar, Danielle Appugliese, Niko Kaciroti, Robert F. Corwyn, and Robert H. Bradley. 2007. "Shorter Sleep Duration Is Associated with Increased Risk for Being Overweight at Ages 9 to 12 Years." *Pediatrics* 120 (5): 1020–29.

Malchiodi, Cathy A., ed. 2011. *Handbook of Art Therapy.* New York: Guilford Press.

———. 2013. *Expressive Therapies.* New York: Guilford Press.

Malchiodi, Cathy A., and David A. Crenshaw. 2015. *Creative Arts and Play Therapy for Attachment Problems.* New York: Guilford Press.

Mann, Dale. 1996. "Serious Play." *Teachers College Record* 97 no. 3 (Spring): 446–69.

Maselko, Joanna, L. Kubzansky, L. Lipsitt, and S. L. Buka. 2011. "Mother's Affection at 8 Months Predicts Emotional Distress in Adulthood." *Journal of Epidemiology & Community Health* 65, no. 7 (July): 621–25. https://doi.org/10.1136/jech.2009.097873.

Masten, Ann S. 2018. "Resilience Theory and Research on Children and Families: Past, Present, and Promise." *Journal of Family Theory & Review* 10 (1): 12–31.

Matheson, Rebecca C. 2016. "DIR Floortime Therapy." Lynchburg College, July 2016. https://www.lynchburg.edu/wp-content/uploads/volume-13-2016/Matheson-Rebecca-DIR-Floortime-Therapy.pdf.

Maxwell, Lorraine. 1999. "Children, Computers, and School Furniture." CEFPI's *Educational Facility Planner* 35 no. 2 (June): 5–7.

Mayfield, Margie I. 2005. "Children's Museums: Purposes, Practices and Play?" *Early Child Development and Care* 175, no. 2 (February): 179–92.

McCabe, Paul C., and Steven R. Shaw, eds. 2010. *Psychiatric Disorders: Current Topics and Interventions for Educators.* Thousand Oaks, CA: Corwin Press.

Mead, George Herbert. 1934. *Mind, Self and Society.* Vol. 111. Chicago: University of Chicago.

Meadan, Hedda, and Brinda Jegatheesan. 2010. "Classroom Pets and Young Children." *Young Children* 65, no. 3 (May): 70–77.

Meares, Russell. 1993. *The Metaphor of Play: Disruption and Restoration in the Borderline Experience.* Northvale, NJ: Jason Aronson.

Meisels, Samuel, J. 1979. *Special Education and Development: Perspectives on Young Children with Special Needs.* Baltimore: University Park Press.

Mendez, Julia L., and Danielle C. Swick. 2018. "Guilford Parent Academy: A Collaborative Effort to Engage Parents in Children's Education." *Education and Treatment of Children* 41, no. 2 (May): 249–68.

Miles, Lisa Rounds. 2009. "The General Store: Reflections on Children at Play." *Young Children* 64, no. 4 (July): 36–41.

Miller, Karen. 2005. *Simple Transitions for Infants and Toddlers.* Silver Spring, MD: Gryphon House.

Milteer, Regina M., Kenneth R. Ginsburg, and Deborah Ann Mulligan. 2012. "The Importance of Play in Promoting Healthy Child Development and Maintaining Strong Parent-Child Bond: Focus on Children in Poverty." *Pediatrics* 129, no. 1 (January): e204–13. https://doi.org/10.1542/peds.2011-2953.

Montessori, Maria. 1967. *The Absorbent Mind.* New York: Henry Holt.

Mooney, Carol Garhart. 2013. *Theories of Childhood: An Introduction to Dewey, Montessori, Erikson, Piaget & Vygotsky.* St. Paul, MN: Redleaf Press.

Moore, Robin C. 1993. *Plants for Play: A Plant Selection Guide for Children's Outdoor Environments.* Berkeley, CA: MIG Communications.

———. 2000. "Childhood's Domain: Play and Place in Child Development." *Michigan Quarterly Review* 39, no. 3 (Summer): 477.

———. 2017. *Childhood's Domain: Play and Place in Child Development*. London: Routledge.

Mow, Evelyn. n.d. "Happy Spaces." https://www.communityplaythings.com/resources/articles/2006/happy-spaces.

Muir, Tracey. 2008. "'Zero Is Not a Number': Teachable Moments and Their Role in Effective Teaching of Numeracy." University of Tasmania, Proceedings of the 31st Annual Conference of the Mathematics Education Research Group of Australasia, edited by M. Goos, R. Brown, and K. Makar, MERGA Inc., 361–67.

National Association of Early Childhood Specialists in State Departments of Education. 2001. *Recess and the Importance of Play. A Position Statement on Young Children and Recess.* NAECS/SDE, Center for At-Risk Education, Colorado State Department of Education, ERIC Clearinghouse.

National Association of Young Children. 2009. Position statement.

National Geographic Society. n.d. "Taking Flight with the Wright Brothers." Accessed October 6, 2020. https://kids.nationalgeographic.com/explore/history/wright-brothers.

O'Connor, Richard. 2020. "Depressed Parents and the Effects on Their Children." Psych Central. Accessed October 2, 2020. https://psychcentral.com/lib/depressed-parents-and-the-effects-on-their-children.

Office of the United Nations High Commissioner for Human Rights. 1989. Convention on the Rights of the Child. General Assembly Resolution 44/25 of 20 November 1989. Accessed June 22, 2006. www.ohchr.org/documents/professionalinterest/crc.pdf.

Olds, Anita Rui. 1979. "Designing Developmentally Optimal Classrooms for Children with Special Needs." In *Special Education and Development: Perspectives on Young Children with Special Needs*, edited by S. J. Meisels. Baltimore: University Park Press.

———. 1989. "Psychological and Physiological Harmony in Child Care Center Design." *Children's Environments Quarterly* 6, no. 4 (Winter): 8–16.

———. 2001. *Child Care Design Guide*. Blacklick, OH: McGraw-Hill.

Olfman, Sharna, ed. 2005. *Childhood Lost: How American Culture Is Failing Our Kids*. Westport, CT: Praeger.

O'Neil, Adrienne, Shae E. Quirk, Siobhan Housden, Sharon L. Brennan, Lana J. Williams, Julie A. Pasco, Michael Berk, and Felice N. Jacka. 2014. "Relationship between Diet and Mental Health in Children and Adolescents: A Systematic Review." *American Journal of Public Health* 104, no. 10 (October): e31–42. https://doi.org/10.2105/AJPH.2014.302110.

Oremland, Evelyn K. 1993. "Abreaction." In *The Therapeutic Powers of Play*, edited by C. E. Schaefer, 143–65. Northvale, NJ: Jason Aronson.

Paes, Veena Mazarello, Ken K. Ong, and Rajalakshmi Lakshman. 2015. "Factors Influencing Obesogenic Dietary Intake in Young Children (0–6 Years): Systematic Review of Qualitative Evidence." *BMJ Open* 5, no. 9 (September): e007396. https://doi.org/10.1136/bmjopen-2014-007396.

Pahl, Kristine M., Paula M. Barrett, and Matthew J. Gullo. 2012. "Examining Potential Risk Factors for Anxiety in Early Childhood." *Journal of Anxiety Disorders* 26, no. 2 (March): 311–20. https://doi.org/10.1016/j.janxdis.2011.12.013.

Paley, Vivian Gussin. 2010. *The Boy on the Beach: Building Community through Play*. Chicago: University of Chicago Press.

Panksepp Jaak, Jeff Burgdorf, Cortney Turner, and Nakia Gordon. 2003. "Modeling ADHD-Type Arousal with Unilateral Frontal Cortex Damage in Rats and Beneficial Effects of Play Therapy." *Brain and Cognition* 52, no. 1 (June): 97–105. https://doi.org/10.1016/s0278-2626(03)00013-7.

Pardee, Mav. 2005. *Community Investment Collaborative for Kids Resource Guide Volume 3: Equipping and Furnishing Early Childhood Facilities.* New York: Local Initiatives Support Corporation/Community Investment Collaborative for Kids. www.lisc.org/media/filer_public/de/b0/deb03f6a-804e-4a0a-8a70-44a99f55c6a3/2005_cick_guide_vol3_equipping.pdf.

Parents for Children's Mental Health. 2013. Parents for Children with Mental Health Factsheet. www.pcmh.ca/factsheets.

Parten, M. B. 1933. "Social Play among Preschool Children." *Journal of Abnormal and Social Psychology* 28 (2): 136–47. https://doi.org/10.1037/h0073939.

Pate, Russell R., Jennifer R. O'Neill, William H. Brown, Karin A. Pfeiffer, Marsha Dowda, and Cheryl L. Addy. 2015. "Prevalence of Compliance with a New Physical Activity Guideline for Preschool-Age Children." *Childhood Obesity* 11, no. 4 (August): 415–20. https://doi.org/10.1089/chi.2014.0143.

Paulus, Frank W., Aline Backes, Charlotte S. Sander, Monika Weber, and Alexander von Gontard. 2015. "Anxiety Disorders and Behavioral Inhibition in Preschool Children: A Population-Based Study." *Child Psychiatry & Human Development* 46, no. 1 (February): 150–57. https://doi.org/10.1007/s10578-014-0460-8.

Pellegrini, Anthony D., and Catherine M. Bohn-Gettler. 2013. "The Benefits of Recess in Primary School." *Scholarpedia* 8 (2): 30,448. https://doi.org/10.4249/scholarpedia.30448.

Perry, Bruce D. 2006. "Applying Principles of Neurodevelopment to Clinical Work with Maltreated and Traumatized Children: The Neurosequential Model of Therapeutics." In *Working with Traumatized Youth in Child Welfare*, edited by Nancy Boyd Webb, 27–52. New York: Guilford Press.

Pica, Rae. 2015. *What If Everybody Understood Child Development? Straight Talk about Bettering Education and Children's Lives*. Thousand Oaks, CA: Corwin Press.

Pichot, Teri. 2012. *Animal-Assisted Brief Therapy: A Solution-Focused Approach*. 2nd ed. New York: Routledge.

Pina-Camacho, L., S. K. Jensen, D. Gaysina, and E. D. Barker. 2015. "Maternal Depression Symptoms, Unhealthy Diet and Child Emotional–Behavioral Dysregulation." *Psychological Medicine* 45, no. 9 (July): 1851–60. https://doi.org/10.1017/S0033291714002955.

Pincus, Donna B., Lauren C. Santucci, Jill T. Ehrenreich, and Sheila M. Eyberg. 2008. "The Implementation of Modified Parent-Child Interaction Therapy for Youth with Separation Anxiety Disorder." *Cognitive and Behavioral Practice* 15, no. 2 (May 1): 118–25. https://doi.org/10.1016/j.cbpra.2007.08.002.

Polanczyk, Guilherme V., Giovanni A. Salum, Luisa S. Sugaya, Arthur Caye, and Luis A. Rohde. 2015. "Annual Research Review: A Meta-Analysis of the Worldwide Prevalence of Mental Disorders in Children and Adolescents." *Journal of Child Psychology and Psychiatry* 56, no. 3 (March): 345–65. https://doi.org/10.1111/jcpp.12381.

Poulou, Maria S. 2015. "Emotional and Behavioral Difficulties in Preschool." *Journal of Child and Family Studies* 24 (2): 225–36.

Powers, Michael. 2018. "The Smallest Remainder: Benjamin and Freud on Play." *MLN* 133 (3): 720–42.

Ray, Dee, and Sue Bratton. 2000. "What the Research Shows about Play Therapy." *International Journal of Play Therapy* 9 (1): 47–88.

Reis, Bruce. 2019. "Creative Repetition." *International Journal of Psychoanalysis* 100 (6): 1306–20.

Rettig, Michael. 2005. "Using the Multiple Intelligences to Enhance Instruction for Young Children and Children with Disabilities." *Early Childhood Education Journal* 32, no. 4 (February): 255–59. https://doi.org/10.1007/s10643-004-0865-2.

Reuille-Dupont, Stacy. 2014. "Impact Psychological Symptom Severity on Leisure Time Exercise Behavior and Perceived Benefits and Barriers to Physical Exercise." PhD diss., The Chicago School of Professional Psychology.

Rivkin, Mary S. 2014. *The Great Outdoors: Advocating for Natural Spaces for Young Children*. Washington, DC: National Association for the Education of Young Children.

Roberts, A., J. Hinds, and P. M. Camic. 2019. "Nature Activities and Wellbeing in Children and Young People: A Systematic Literature Review." *Journal of Adventure Education and Outdoor Learning* 20 (4): 298–318.

Rose, Karole A.. 2020. "Quieting the Buzz: Drama Therapy and Mindfulness in the Classroom, An Intervention." MA thesis, Lesley University, Cambridge, MA: DigitalCommons@Lesley.

Ross, Gena L. 2018. "Kansas City, Missouri, Inner City Schools' Parent Involvement Policy, Practices, and Accreditation Problems." PhD diss., Walden Dissertations and Doctoral Studies, 4754. https://scholarworks.waldenu.edu/dissertations/4754.

Rubin, Kenneth H., Robert J. Coplan, and Julie C. Bowker. 2009. "Social Withdrawal in Childhood." *Annual Review of Psychology* 60: 141–71. https://doi.org/10.1146/annurev.psych.60.110707.163642.

Sahlberg, Pasi, and William Doyle. 2019. *Let the Children Play: How More Play Will Save Our Schools and Help Children Thrive*. Oxford: Oxford University Press.

Salcuni, Silvia, Daniela Di Riso, Diana Mabilia, and Adriana Lis. 2017. "Psychotherapy with a 3-Year-Old Child: The Role of Play in the Unfolding Process." *Frontiers in Psychology* 7, art. 2021. https://doi.org/10.3389/fpsyg.2016.02021.

Schaefer, Charles E., ed. 1993. *The Therapeutic Powers of Play*. Northvale, NJ: Jason Aronson.

———. 1999. "Curative Factors in Play Therapy." *Journal for the Professional Counselor* 14, no. 1 (Spring): 7–16.

———. 2001. "Prescriptive Play Therapy." *International Journal of Play Therapy* 10 (2): 57–73. http://dx.doi.org/10.1037/h0089480.

Schaefer, Charles E., and Donna M. Cangelosi, eds. 2002. *Play Therapy Techniques*. Northvale, NJ: Jason Aronson.

Schaefer, Charles E., and Athena A. Drewes. 2009. "The Therapeutic Powers of Play and Play Therapy." In *Blending Play Therapy with Cognitive Behavioral Therapy: Evidence-Based and Other Effective Treatments and Techniques*, edited by Athena A. Drewes, 3–15. Hoboken, NJ: John Wiley and Sons.

———. 2011. "The Therapeutic Powers of Play and Play Therapy" in *School-Based Play Therapy*, 2nd ed., edited by Athena A. Drewes and Charles E. Schaefer. Hoboken, NJ: John Wiley and Sons. https://doi.org/10.1002/9781118269701.ch1.

Serafini, Gianluca, Xenia Gonda, Maurizio Pompili, Zoltan Rihmer, Mario Amore, and Batya Engel-Yeger. 2016. "The Relationship between Sensory Processing Patterns, Alexithymia, Traumatic Childhood Experiences, and Quality of Life among Patients with Unipolar and Bipolar Disorders." *Child Abuse & Neglect* 62 (December): 39–50. https://doi.org/10.1016/j.chiabu.2016.09.013.

Shamir-Essakow, Galia, Judy A. Ungerer, and Ronald M. Rapee. 2005. "Attachment, Behavioral Inhibition, and Anxiety in Preschool Children." *Journal of Abnormal Child Psychology* 33, no. 2 (April): 131–43.

Shell, Ellen Ruppel. 1994. "Kids Don't Need Equipment, They Need Opportunity." *Smithsonian Magazine* 25, no. 4 (July): 78–87.

Shrinivasa, Basavaraj, Madina Bukhari, G. Ragesh, and Ameer Hamza. 2018. "Therapeutic Intervention for Children through Play: An Overview." *Archives of Mental Health* 19, no. 2 (July–December): 82.

Smith, Bradley H., Gulden Esat, and Anjali Kanojia. 2020. "School-Based Yoga for Managing Stress and Anxiety." In *Applying Psychology in the Schools. Promoting Mind-Body Health in Schools: Interventions for Mental Health Professionals*, edited by C. Maykel and M. A. Bray, 201–16. Washington, DC: American Psychological Association. https://doi.org/10.1037/0000157-014.

Steiner, Hans, ed. 1997. *Treating Preschool Children*. San Francisco: Jossey-Bass.

Stormont, Melissa, Keith C. Herman, and Wendy M. Reinke. 2015. "The Overlooked Children: How Teachers Can Support Children with Internalizing Behaviors." *Beyond Behavior* 24 (2): 39–45. https://doi.org/10.1177/107429561502400206.

Subbarayan, A., B. Ganesan, Anbumani, and Jayanthini. 2008. "Temperamental Traits of Breath Holding Children: A Case Control Study." *Indian Journal of Psychiatry* 50, no. 3 (July–September): 192–96. https://doi.org/10.4103/0019-5545.43635.

Sutton-Smith, Brian. 2009. *The Ambiguity of Play*. Cambridge, MA: Harvard University Press.

Szekely, Amanda, Therese Ahlers, Julie Cohen, and Cindy Oser. 2018. "Advancing Infant and Early Childhood Mental Health: The Integration of DC: 0–5™ into State Policy and Systems." *ZERO TO THREE* 39, no. 2 (November): 27–35.

Thompson, Ross A., Rebecca Goodwin, and Sara Meyer. 2006. "Social Development, Psychological Understanding, Self-Understanding, and Relationships." In *Handbook of Preschool Mental Health: Development, Disorders, and Treatment*, edited by Joan L. Luby, 3–22. New York: Guilford Press.

Thompson, Sharon D. 1994. "What's a Clothesline Doing on the Playground?" *Young Children* 50, no. 1 (November): 70–71.

Thompson, Stacy D., and Jill M. Raisor. 2013. "Meeting the Sensory Needs of Young Children." *Young Children* 68, no. 2 (May): 34–40, 42–43.

Timmons, Brian W., Patti-Jean Naylor, and Karin A. Pfeiffer. 2007. "Physical Activity for Preschool Children—How Much and How?" *Applied Physiology, Nutrition, and Metabolism* 32 (S2E): S122–34.

Torquati, Julia, Mary M. Gabriel, Julie Jones-Branch, and J. Leeper-Miller. 2010. "A Natural Way to Nurture Children's Development and Learning." *Young Children* 65, no. 6 (November): 98–104.

Turner, Pauline H., and Tommie J. Hamner. 1994. *Child Development and Early Education: Infancy through Preschool*. Boston: Allyn and Bacon.

U.N. General Assembly. 1989. "Convention on the Rights of the Child." *United Nations, Treaty Series* 1577, no. 3.

US Department of Health and Human Services, Office of Disease Prevention and Health Promotion. 2020. "Healthy People 2020." www.healthypeople.gov/2020/topics-objectives.

Van Andel, Joost. 1990. "Places Children Like, Dislike, and Fear." *Children's Environments Quarterly* 7 (4): 24–31.

Van Der Kolk, Bessel A. 2005. "Developmental Trauma Disorder: Toward a Rational Diagnosis for Children with Complex Trauma Histories." *Psychiatric Annals* 35, no. 5 (May): 401–8. https://doi.org/10.3928/00485713-20050501-06.

Waelder, Robert. 1933. "The Psychoanalytic Theory of Play." *The Psychoanalytic Quarterly* 2 (2): 208–24. https://doi.org/10.1080/21674086.1933.11925173.

Wagenfeld, Amy. 2005. *Foundations of Pediatric Practice for the Occupational Therapy Assistant*. Thorofare, NJ: Slack.

Wallach, Michael A., and Nathan Kogan. 1965. *Modes of Thinking in Young Children*. New York: Holt, Rinehart and Winston.

Waltz, Megan. 2013. "The Importance of Social and Emotional Development in Young Children." St. Paul, MN.

Webb, James T., Edward R. Amend, Nadia E. Webb, Jean Goerss, Paul Beljan, and F. Richard Olenchak. 2016. *Misdiagnosis and Dual Diagnoses of Gifted Children and Adults: ADHD, Bipolar, OCD, Asperger's, Depression, and Other Disorders*, 2nd ed. Scottsdale, AZ: Great Potential Press.

Wells, Nancy M. 2000. "At Home with Nature: Effects of 'Greenness' on Children's Cognitive Functioning." *Environment and Behavior* 32, no. 6 (November 1): 775–95. https://doi.org/10.1177/00139160021972793.

Wells, Nancy M., and Gary W. Evans. 2003. "Nearby Nature: A Buffer of Life Stress among Rural Children." *Environment and Behavior* 35, no. 3 (May 1): 311–330. https://doi.org/10.1177/0013916503035003001.

Western Center for Research and Education on Violence Against Women and Children. 2017. "What Does It Mean to Be Culturally Competent?" *Make It Our Business* blog. June 22. makeitourbusiness.ca/blog/what-does-it-mean-be-culturally-competent.

Whalen, Diana J., Chad M. Sylvester, and Joan L. Luby. 2017. "Depression and Anxiety in Preschoolers: A Review of the Past 7 Years." *Child and Adolescent Psychiatric Clinics* 26 (3): 503–22. https://doi.org/10.1016/j.chc.2017.02.006.

White, Randy. 2004. "Young Children's Relationship with Nature: Its Importance to Children's Development & the Earth's Future." White Hutchinson Leisure & Learning Group, 1–9.

White, Randy, and Vicki Stoecklin. 1998. "Children's Outdoor Play and Learning Environments: Returning to Nature." March/April. White Hutchinson Leisure & Learning Group.

Whitney, Daniel G., and Mark D. Peterson. 2019. "U.S. National and State-Level Prevalence of Mental Health Disorders and Disparities of Mental Health Care Use in Children." *JAMA Pediatrics* 173 (4): 389–91.

Wien, Carol Anne, Annette Coates, Bobbi-Lynn Keating, and Barbara Christine Bigelow. 2005. "Designing the Environment to Build Connection to Place." *Young Children* 60, no. 3 (May): 16–24.

Williams, Katherine. 2000. "Childhood Revealed: Art Expressing Pain, Discovery and Hope." *American Journal of Art Therapy* 39, no. 2 (November): 67.

Wilson, Penny. 2010. *The Playwork Primer*. College Park, MD: Alliance for Childhood. https://files.eric.ed.gov/fulltext/ED511455.pdf.

Winnicott, Donald W. 1971. *Playing and Reality*. London: Tavistock.

Wolf, Gregory K., Matthew Reinhard, Louis J. Cozolino, Alex Caldwell, and Joy K. Asamen. 2009. "Neuropsychiatric Symptoms of Complex Posttraumatic Stress Disorder: A Preliminary Minnesota Multiphasic Personality Inventory Scale to Identify Adult Survivors of Childhood Abuse." *Psychological Trauma: Theory, Research, Practice, and Policy* 1, no. 1 (March): 49–64.

Wolpe, Joseph. 1958. *Psychotherapy by Reciprocal Inhibition*. Stanford, CA: Stanford University Press.

Woltmann, Adolf, G. 1960. "Spontaneous Puppetry by Children as a Projective Method." In *Projective Techniques with Children*, edited by Albert I. Rabin and Mary Robbins Haworth, 305–12. New York: Grune and Stratton.

Yogman, Michael, Andrew Garner, Jeffrey Hutchinson, Kathy Hirsh-Pasek, Roberta Michnick Golinkoff, and Committee on Psychosocial Aspects of Child and Family Health. 2018. "The Power of Play: A Pediatric Role in Enhancing Development in Young Children." *Pediatrics* 142, no. 3.

Zarei, Kasra. 2020. "How Coronavirus and Civil Unrest Put Children's Health at Risk" *The Philadelphia Inquirer*. June 12.

Index

action signs
  anxiety, 69–70
  basic facts about, 24
  defined, 8
  for depression, 63–64
adaptive play tools, 17, 76–77
adverse childhood experiences (ACEs)
  anxiety and, 70
  cathartic powers of play to combat, 76, 77
  consequences of, 34
  defined, 33
  depression and, 63
  examples of, 32, 33
  handout for understanding, 34, 170
  impact of, on development, 41
  importance of understanding neurophysiological processes resulting from, 20
  SPD and, 5
  transitioning and, 106
  using specific play tools and, 129
American Academy of Neurology, 148
American Academy of Pediatrics (AAP), 36, 84, 86, 100–101
American Dance Therapy Association, 148
American Music Association, 148
American Psychiatric Association, 6, 60, 67
anger management skills, 54
animals, 163–164, 165
anxiety
  ACEs and, 70
  action signs for, 69–70
  characteristics, 61, 67–69
  depression and, 5
  DSM and, 67
  EIIPS and, 67
  GAD and, 68
  Jessica, 65–66, 71
  music and movement and, 152
  SPD and, 5
  types, 67
attachments
  characteristics of secure, 44
  extreme, as characteristic of anxiety, 68
  importance of secure, 14, 16, 42–43
  poor, 45, 63
attention deficit hyperactivity disorder (ADHD), 5
autonomy, cultivating, 114–116
Axline, Virginia, 101

backpack story packs, 153
baking and cooking, 165–167
Bao, Yanping, 33
behaviors
  child's definition of environment's sensory input and, 105
  criteria for determining challenging versus diagnosable, 37
  encouraging
    for developing healthy social skills, 53, 54
    for emotional regulation, 47, 50
  externalizing, ix, 3–4
  families as models for, 33–34
  inhibited, and anxiety, 69–70
  variables in interpreting, 21–23
  See also internalizing behaviors
blocks, 97, 144
boat play, 141–142
body language, 52
Bookwalter, Julie, 144
boundaries
  importance of, 114
  in outdoor environment, 115–116
  predictability and, 116
brain
  early experiences and architecture of, 15, 43
  environment and, 104
  flexibility of, 101
  movement and, 104
breathing techniques, 51
Brown, Stuart, 1–2, 81
buddying up children, 55
The Bumblebee Waggle, 89

cardboard boxes, 126, 127
cardboard cities, 126
caregivers. *See* families
Carle, Eric, 154
cathartic powers of play
  accelerates child development, 83
  accesses unconscious, 79
  builds identity, 83
  to combat ACEs, 76, 77
  counters stress, 81
  creates bonds, 80
  drives creativity, 2, 83, 88
  empowers problem solving, 82
  encourages empathy, 83
  in Freud's psychodynamic theory of play, 17, 28–29, 75
  ideas for using nature, 140–144
  improves physical health, 83
  learning skills and concepts, 79
  mental wellness and, 17, 84
  nurtures competence, 81

pathways to creativity and, 147
permits make-believe, 83
permits storytelling, 79
promotes resilience, 80
regulates emotions, 81–82
as rehearsal for social competencies, 83
relearning maladaptive skills, 80
self-expression, 78
self-healing through, 79
shapes values, 80
strengthens self-regulation, 81
transcends barriers, 80
See also pathways to creativity

Centers for Disease Control and Prevention (CDC), 36

center stage, building, 56

child
defined, 8
focus on whole, 77

child development
contacting professionals about, 39
defined, 8
fantasy play and, 92
impact of ACEs on, 41
internalizing behaviors and, 77
milestones for
by age eight, 102, 103
awareness of strengths and weaknesses, 39–41
child's life experiences and, 36
family's culture and language and, 35
growth charts for, 36
influences on, 40
social and emotional, 103
understanding, 35–36
play accelerates, 83
reaching full potential, 101
stages of, 92
theoretical principles
basic facts about, 27
prepared environment for play, 26, 28, 101
psychodynamic theory of play, 17, 26, 28–29, 75
psychosocial development theory, 26, 29–30, 92, 102

Childhood and Society (Erikson), 29

Childhood's Domain: Play and Place in Child Development (Moore), 125

child temperament scale, handout, 6, 170

choice, as motivator, 117

clothesline play, 142

color
in natural world, 140
as pathway to creativity, 163
as visual organizer, 114, 115

communication
between child and caregiver, 43
cultural competence and, 38
developing child's conversation skills, 52
direct individualization and, 18
handout for effective, between stakeholders and families, 25, 170
importance of allowing children to express emotions safely and freely, 14
importance of consistent and understandable, among all stakeholders, 24
as key for direct individualization, 18
nonverbal, 51, 52
play as tool of, 76, 78

competence
foster security, 111
play nurtures, 81, 110–111

conflict resolution skills, 48

constructive play, 95–97

cooking and baking, 165–167

cooperative play
benefits of, 93
emphasizing, 55
project ideas, 93, 94–95

COVID-19, quarantining and social restrictions during, 33

Creative Arts and Play Therapy for Attachment Problems (Malchiodi and Crenshaw), x

creativity
color as pathway to, 163
as component of successful prescriptive tool kit, 76
fantasy play builds, 88
importance of, in early childhood curricula, 126, 129
outdoor play spaces for inspiring, 137–138, 140
play increases, 2, 83, 88
play tools for encouraging, 127–128
richness in environment and, 121
See also pathways to creativity

Crenshaw, David, x

Csikszentmihalyi, Mihaly, 19

cultural competence
factors to consider, 38
handout of family questionnaire, 24, 38, 170
strategies for, 37

Danoff-Burg, James, 89

depression (clinical) in preschoolers
action signs, 63–64
anxiety and, 5
characteristics, 60–61, 62–63
determining characteristics of each child's, 59
DSM and, 60
prevalence, 4
SPD and, 5
Wally, 58–60, 64

developmental level and interpreting behaviors, 22, 23

Diagnostic and Statistical Manual of Mental Disorders (DSM-5) (American Psychiatric Association), 6, 60, 67

direct individualization, as accommodating child's unique formula, 18

direct spatial prompts, 52
discovery play, 143–144
displays of children's work, 120
distress and internalizing behaviors, 2
dollhouses, 91
drawing, 150–151
dress-up play, benefits of, 90
Drewes, Athena A., 79
Duncan, Sandra, 16–17

eating habits and depression, 62–63
educators. *See* stakeholders
Eight Ages of Man (Erikson), 29
EIIPS (early identification, intervention, primary prevention, and support of internalizing behaviors)
 anxiety and, 67
 components to consider, 41
 depression and, 60
 importance of, x
 pathways to creativity and, 147, 148–149
 play tool kit, 112
 stakeholders' partnerships with families, 6–7, 129
Eisen, George, 86
emotional challenges, play and, 2
emotional development. *See* mental wellness
emotional literacy, building, 50
emotional regulation
 components of, 45
 mental wellness and, 45–46
 play and, xii, 80
 prompts to support, 52
 secure attachments and, 42–43, 44
 storytelling and, 152
 strategies to improve child's, 46, 47–51, 52, 171
emotions
 communication of, through play, 17
 importance of allowing children to express, safely and freely, 14
 play regulates, 81–82
 using music and, 124, 157
empathy, 50, 54, 83
environment
 boundaries in
  importance of, 114
  outdoor areas, 115–116
  predictability and, 116
 brain and, 104
 characteristics of, supportive of internalizing behaviors, 17, 102–104, 116
 children's needs in play spaces, 122–124
 child's unique formula and, 101–102
 choice in, 117
 compatibility of child's temperament with, 6
 components of, 16–17
 creating behavior expectations in, 47
 creative bakery play space, 166
 cultivating independence and autonomy, 114–116
 defined, 8
 elements of, promoting competence, 110–111
 as enforcing expectation of organization, 116
 essential features of, 14
 incorporating movement into, 104–105
 interpreting behaviors and, 22
 mental wellness and, 101
 in Montessori theory, 26, 28, 101
 play tools effectively integrating into, 117–120
 privacy and solitude in, 124–125
 processing styles of information from, 107
  low-registering, 107–108
  sensory avoidance, 108–109
  sensory seeking, 109–110
  sensory sensitivity, 110
 quiet play area, 96
 richness in, 120–121
 sensory break spaces, 163
 sensory stimulation and, 105–107
 sound's impact on, 122
 uninterrupted exploration of, 102
 See also nature / natural world
Erikson, Erik
 dollhouses and, 91
 fantasy play and development of child, 92
 play as important for children to develop competence, 110–111
 psychosocial development theory, 26, 29–30, 92, 102
 self-healing through play, 79
evaluations
 goal of mental wellness, 25
 level of impairment and, 23–24
Evolutionary Playwork and Reflective Analytic Practice (Hughes), 85
externalizing behaviors
 described, ix
 internalizing behaviors compared to, 3–4

families
 anxiety and controlling or overprotective, 70
 as behavioral models, 33–34
 children without consistent primary caregiver, 45
 communication between child and, 43
 culture and language of, 22, 35
 handout for preparing for appointment with professionals about child's development, 39, 170
 history of mental health challenges, 63
 importance of secure, 42–43
 involvement of
  defined, 8
  forms of, 112
  handout for importance of, 112, 171
  strategies to encourage, 113

questionnaire to help stakeholders with child's unique formula, 24, 38, 170
risk for anxiety disorders and, 69
stakeholders' partnerships with
education about importance of secure attachments, 16
effective communication handout, 25, 170
EIIPS and, 6–7, 129
importance of consistent and understandable communication, 24
storytelling with, 153

family theme bags, 153

fantasy play, 48, 88–92

fears, conquering through play, 17

flexibility
of brain, 101
as component of successful prescriptive tool kit, 76
play and, 80
richness in environment and, 121

"flow," 19

Fraiberg, Selma, 32

Freud, Sigmund
accessing unconscious through play, 79
children's determination to be competent, 110
literature in development of child, 151
play and transference, 28, 80, 129
psychodynamic theory of play, 17, 26, 28–29, 75
relearning maladaptive skills through play, 80

friendships and play, xii

Froebel, Friedrich, 76, 78

gadget play, 142–143

gardening, 164–165

Gardner, Howard, 20, 21

generalized anxiety disorder (GAD), 68
See also anxiety

Gerke, Pamela, 151

gestural prompts, 52

giftedness and depression, 63

Ginsburg, Kenneth R., x

goodness of fit, 6, 170

Gray, Peter, 1–2

Hannaford, Carla, 104

Harvard Medical School, x

Haughey, Sally, 16–17

helplessness and anxiety, 61

house play, benefits of, 90

Huang, Xiaolin, 33

Hughes, Bob, 85

identity, 83, 88

imagination. *See* creativity

"I" messages, 54

impulsiveness and anxiety, 70

independence, cultivating, 83, 114–116, 140

indirect verbal prompts, 52

individuality. *See* unique formula

innovation and play, 85

insomnia, as characteristic of anxiety, 68

Institute of Medicine, 86

instructional strategies, handout for, 110, 171

internalizing behaviors
characteristics of environment supportive of, 17, 102–104, 116
child development and, 77
comorbidities, 5–6
considerations for play spaces and, 120–121, 122–123
cooperative play and, 93
described, ix, 2, 4
externalizing behaviors compared to, 3–4
fantasy play and, 88–89
importance of early identification of, x
need for security and, 111
physical play and, 86
pillars of addressing
1. early identification, intervention, and prevention, 14, 15–16
2. secure relational attachments, 14, 16
3. environment with essential needs, 14, 16–17
4. diverse play menu, 14–15, 17–18
5. direct individualization, 15, 18
play and, 2
play tools and, 104, 160, 163
prevalence, 4
psychodynamic theory of play, 75
secure attachments, emotional regulation and, 42–43
styles of processing environmental information, 107
low-registering, 107–108
sensory avoidance, 108–109
sensory seeking, 109–110
sensory sensitivity, 110
using nature to prevent and address, 141–144
See also pathways to creativity

intervention methods, individualization of, 15–16

irritability, 62

Jensen, Eric, 104

Keeler, Rusty, 134

kindness, 53

Kranowitz, Carol, 6

Landalf, Helen, 151

language skills and play, xii, 2, 79, 83

Last Child in the Woods (Louv), x

learning
  handout for style and multiple intelligences, 20, 170
  movement and, 18, 134
  requires children's emotional engagement with teachers, 111
  through play, 79

Leichter-Saxby, Morgan, 125

listening skills, 52, 88

Liu, Jia Jia, 33

Louv, Richard, x

Lu, Lin, 33

The Magic of the Stump Pile (Bookwalter and Vicqueneau), 144

magnification play, 141

make-believe, play permits, 83

Make Me a Machine game, 89

Malchiodi, Cathy, x

Martin, Jody, 16–17

mazes, 144

McCabe, Paul C., 147

mental wellness
  cathartic powers of play and, 17, 84
  defined, 8
  developmental level and, 23
  diverse, individualized play menu as necessary for, 14–15
  emotional regulation and, 45–46
  environment and, 101
  goal of evaluations, 25
  social skills and, 46

Montessori, Maria
  environment's sensory stimulation, 105
  importance of animals, 163–164
  prepared environment for play theory, 26, 28, 101

Mood Music technique, 157

Moore, Robin, 125

motivation, handout for fostering intrinsic, 56, 171

movement
  brain and, 104
  break ideas, 89
  creative, as effective for, transitioning, 105
  handout for creative, 105, 171
  importance of, in learning, 18
  incorporating, into environment, 104–105
  learning with, 134
  with music, 152, 155–156
  in outdoor play spaces, 134–136
  in storytelling, 151, 159

Movement Stories for Young Children: Ages 3–6 (Landalf and Gerke), 151

multiple intelligences, 20, 21, 170

music
  handout with suggestions for, 156, 172
  with movement, 152, 155–156
  storytelling through, 151
  using to explore emotions, 124, 157

National Art Education Association, 126, 129

National Association for the Education of Young Children, 126, 129

National Institute of Mental Health (NIMH), 147

National Toy Hall of Fame, 126

Natural Playscapes: Creating Outdoor Play Environments for the Soul (Keeler), 134

nature / natural world
  benefits of, 49, 83, 129, 132
  boundaries in, for play, 115–116
  child-preferred play spaces in, 132–143
  color in, 140
  footpaths in, 134, 136
  gardening, 164–165
  healing elements of, 77, 140
  ideas for cathartic play in, 140–144
  ideas for tools and structures, 54
  indoor ideas to expose child to, 131
  as integral part of curriculum, 77–78, 130
  open-ended materials and features in, 133
  open-ended play in, 132
  play spaces for
    inspiring creativity, 137–138, 140
    physical activity, 134–136
    quiet retreat, 136–137
  power of plants, 139
  rainy-day play, 138, 140
  risk-taking and, 132, 140
  sound to complement play in, 134, 137

neuroplasticity, 15, 16, 43

noise level, 122

nutrition, poor, 62–63, 70

obsessive-compulsive disorder (OCD). *See* anxiety

Olds, Anita, 122

One Place for Special Needs (website), 151

Out-of-Sync Child (Kranowitz), 6

painting, 150–151

panic disorder. *See* anxiety

parenting styles and anxiety, 70

Parents for Children's Mental Health, 7

partnering children, 55

pathways to creativity
  cathartic value of, 147
  cooking and baking, 165–167
  EIIPS and, 147, 148–149

forms and delivery methods of
basic facts about, 146, 148
drawing and painting, 150–151
gardening, 164–165
music and movement, 152, 155–156
puppets, 153, 156–159
storytelling, 151–152, 153
handout for tools for play spaces, creative pathways, and self-expression, 126, 171
as integral part of curriculum, 149
miniature play tools, 160
movement in storytelling, 151, 159
pets, 163–164, 165
processes, 149
recommendations for, 148
sensory, 160–163
yoga, 164

pets, 163–164, 165

physical activity outdoors, 134–136

physical health
complaints about, 62, 67–68
play improves, 83

physical play, 86, 88

Pica, Rae, 31–32

play
basic facts about, ix
as communication tool, 76
constructive, 95–96, 97
cooperative, 55, 93–96
defined, 8
diverse, individualized menus of, 14–15, 17–18
as enhancing children's competence, 110
fantasy, 48, 88–92
importance of, x, 41
importance of varied menu of, 114
innovation and, 85
internalizing behaviors and, 2
mastery element of, 28–29
menus, 51–52, 87
in natural world as integral part of curriculum, 77–78
neuroplasticity and, 16
nurtures competence, 81, 110–111
open-ended, in nature, 132
open-ended and mobile materials as best, 76–77
physical, 86, 88
prescriptive approach to, 76
pretend, 83
problem solving and, 2, 80, 82, 88
psychodynamic theory of, 17, 28–29
quiet, 96–98
rainy-day play in nature, 138, 140
sensory, 48
skills developed through, xii, 2, 80, 83
social skills and, x, 51
survival and, 86
transference and, 28, 80, 129
as UN recognized right of every child, 75
varying type of, 81
whole-child approach, 17
as "the work of the child" in prepared environment theory of, 28
See also cathartic powers of play

"Play, Spirit, and Character" (Brown), 81

Play Everything (blog by Leichter-Saxby), 125

play spaces, children's needs in, 122–124

play tools
ACEs and using specific, 129
adaptive, 17, 76–77
basic facts about, 117
blocks, 97
constructive, 96
effectively integrating in environment, 117–120
EIIPS kit, 112
for encouraging creativity, 127–128
fantasy play, 88, 91
handout for ideas for, 126, 171
handout for sensory, 163, 172
internalizing behaviors and, 104, 160, 163
organization and availability of, 116
for promoting quiet play, 98
rotating choice, 117

pleasure and depression, 62

positive affirmations, 50

positive reinforcement, 52

positive self-talk, 55

post-traumatic stress disorder (PTSD). *See* anxiety

"The Power of Play: A Pediatric Role in Enhancing the Development in Young Children" (AAP), 100–101

predictability, 116–117

prepared environment for play theory, 26, 28, 101

preschoolers
percent meeting criteria for diagnosable condition, 1
stakeholders eating lunch with, 18

privacy, 124–125

problem solving and play, 2, 80, 82, 88

prompts to support emotional regulation, 52

Psychiatric Disorders: Current Topics and Interventions for Educators (McCabe and Shaw), 147

Psychodynamic Theory of Play (Freud), 17, 26, 28–29, 75

psychological first aid, 33

psychosocial development theory, 26, 29–30, 92, 102

puppets, 153, 156–159

quiet play, 96–98

reciprocal inhibition, 81

recovery, 19

redirection, 50

relaxation techniques, 51

"repetition compulsion," 29, 79

repetitive activities, 48

resilience, 80

restorative healing process, described, 19

risk factors. *See* action signs

risk-taking, nature as promoting, 132, 140

Rivkin, Mary S., 81

role-play, 53, 54, 80

rotating resource library, 153

routines, 102, 116, 117

sadness, 62

Schaefer, Charles E., 79

schedules, 102, 116, 117

self-confidence
- internalizing behaviors and, 2
- music and movement and, 152
- play and, xii
- puppets and, 156
- storytelling and, 151

self-esteem, building child's, 54

self-expression. *See* creativity

self-reflection and play, 83

self-regulation
- defined, 81
- play teaches, 81–82
- sensory stimulation and, 107
- *See also* emotional regulation

self-talk
- negative, and depression and anxiety and, 61
- positive, 55
- pretend play and, 83

self-worth, ways to let child individually shine, 19

senses / sensory systems, 114
- anxiety and, 69
- effect on child's system, 7
- environment
  - allowing personalized stimulation, 14
  - incorporating each sense into, 108–109
  - promoting child's control over amount of stimulation in, 114
  - sound's impact on, 122
  - stimulating each, in, 105–107
- incorporating, into daily activities and environment, 108–109
- music and movement, 124, 152
- as part of child's unique formula, 6
- as pathways to creativity, 160–163
- processing
  - anxiety and, 70
  - issues, 6
  - low-registering pattern, 107–108
  - sensory-avoiding pattern, 108–109
  - sensory-seeking pattern, 109–110
  - sensory-sensitive pattern, 110
- self-regulation and stimulation of, 107
- sound to complement outdoor play, 134, 137
- stimulating, in natural world, 140
- *See also* color

sensory play, 48

sensory processing disorder (SPD), formerly sensory integration disorder (SID), 5–6

separation anxiety and separation anxiety disorder (SAD), 23, 68
- *See also* anxiety

Shaw, Steven R., 147

Shi, Jie, 33

sleep difficulties, as characteristic of anxiety, 68–69

sleep disruption, depression, 62

social challenges
- anxiety and, 70
- depression and anxiety and, 61, 64
- play and, 2, 80

social competencies and play, xii, 83

social development. *See* mental wellness

social experiences, offering variety of, 56

social phobia, 68
- *See also* anxiety

social skills
- handout for literature to develop, 154, 172
- mental wellness and, 46
- play strengthens, 80
- puppets and, 153, 156
- strategies to strengthen, 51–56

social stories, 151

solitary play, 96–98

somatic complaints
- characteristic of anxiety, 67–68
- depression, 62

spatial prompts, 52

stakeholders
- characteristics of quality educators, 111
- defined, 9
- eating lunch with preschoolers, 18
- establishing trust with children, 49, 55
- expected behaviors modeled by, 47, 50, 53, 54
- handout for tools for play spaces, creative pathways and self-expression, 126, 171
- handout for understanding ACEs, 34, 170
- importance of, allowing children to express emotions safely and freely, 14
- modeling actions for effective transitioning, 106
- need to emotionally engage children, 111
- partnerships between families and
  - education about importance of secure attachments, 16
  - effective communication handout, 25, 170

EIIPS and, 6–7, 129
importance of consistent and understandable communication, 24
providing physical support, 50
schedules and routines, 116, 117102
Stixrud, William, 77
storybooks, illustrated, 154
storytelling
importance of, 79
with movement, 151, 159
as pathway to creativity, 151–152, 153
through music, 151
stressors
play as counter to toxicity of, 81
secure attachments as buffer to, 43

temperament
defined, 9
handout, 170
types, at risk for depression, 63
terminology, 8–9
themed fantasy play, 91–92
theory, defined, 26
Theory of Psychosocial Development (Erikson), 29, 92
"The Therapeutic Powers of Play and Play Therapy" (Schaefer and Drewes), 79
thought patterns, retraining, 55
"tinker" toys, 144
transference, play as useful means of, 28, 80, 129
transitioning
creative movement as effective for, 105
handout with suggestions for, 106, 171
modeling actions for effective, 106
trench play, 141
trust
allowing children to express emotions safely and freely, 14
emotional regulation and, 49
in Erikson's psychosocial development theory, 29, 30
play and, xii
secure attachments and, 14, 16, 42
stakeholders establishing, with children, 49, 55

unique formula
defined, 19
direct individualization as accommodating, 18
elements of, 19–20
environment and child's, 101–102
handout for questionnaire for family to help stakeholders with child's unique formula, 24, 38, 170
importance of identifying child's, 20
interpreting behaviors and, 22
restorative healing process and, 19
sensory processing issues and, 6

values, play shapes, 80
Vicqueneau, Veronika, 144
visual aids
color as organizer, 114, 115
creating behavior expectations using, 47

warning signs. *See* action signs
What If Everybody Understood Child Development? (Pica), 31–32
Where Do the Children Play? (PBS documentary), 126
withdrawal and anxiety, 70
wood bench play, 142
work of children, displaying, 120
Wright brothers, 85

yoga, 164